DEBRETT'S

GUIDE TO
BUSINESS
ETIQUETTE

Debrett's Guide to Business Etiquette
Published by Debrett's Limited
www.debretts.com
Copyright © Debrett's Limited 2021

Text: Elizabeth Wyse
Additional text: Rupert Wesson
Editorial: Lucy Hume
Designer: Karen Wilks

Illustrations on pages 8, 12, 15, 31, 42, 54, 62, 68, 92, 109, 112, 114, 115, 118, 125, 129, 139, 144, 152, 155, 163, 166, 167, 175, 176, 179, 184, 188, 190, 193, 198, 206, 213 © Shutterstock. All other illustrations © 4D2A.

All rights reserved. No part of this publication may be reproduced, stored in a retrieval system, or transmitted in any form or by any means, without the prior permission of the publisher, nor be otherwise circulated in any form of binding or cover other than that in which it is published and without similar condition being imposed on the subsequent purchaser.

ISBN 978-1-9997670-8-2

Printed and bound by L.E.G.O. Group, Italy

GUIDE TO
BUSINESS
ETIQUETTE

THE DIFFICULTY
LIES NOT SO
MUCH IN
DEVELOPING
NEW IDEAS AS
IN ESCAPING
FROM OLD
ONES.

John Maynard Keynes

Contents

Foreword by Lord Bilimoria of Chelsea CBE, DL	06
01.	Office Working and Home Working	08
02.	Job Applications	18
03.	Introductions	34
04.	Office Manners	42
05.	Punctuality	56
06.	Office Dress	62
07.	Office Relationships	68
08.	Office Social Life	82
09.	Private vs Public	92
10.	Communications in the Office	98
11.	Telephone Etiquette	106
12.	Email Communication	114
13.	Business Correspondence	120
14.	Reports and Reviews	130
15.	Problem-Solving Procedures	136
16.	Meetings	152
17.	Public Speaking and Presentations	166
18.	Soft Skills	184
19.	Communication Styles	198
20.	Networking and Relationship Building	206
21.	Business Entertaining and Travel	212
Afterword	220
Index	222

Foreword

Good manners are not just good – not just the right thing to do – but good for business.

The Covid-19 pandemic, including workplace restrictions, has caused unparalleled disruption to businesses' ways of working, driving significant behavioural changes amongst all types of workers. The etiquette landscape has changed, with the most basic norms such as an office-based working week and shaking hands being questioned. The etiquette landscape is more diverse and more important to understand than ever before – *Debrett's Guide to Business Etiquette* comes at this crucial time.

The pandemic has not only separated us from loved ones and business partners and restricted our physical access to travel around the world, but it has also dramatically increased our awareness of the wellbeing of others. We have seen communities and countries rally together like never before, showing our increased awareness of others; this along with an ability to make others comfortable and feel valued defines good manners and etiquette.

Good manners, decorum, respect and courtesy will open doors that education alone cannot. We live in a competitive world where good etiquette and being at ease with both colleagues and clients are essential ways of gaining an advantage. There are many drivers to business success including intelligence and educational achievements, but combining these with good manners will help you build all types of connections.

Digitisation has brought about new social situations, where even the individuals with the most advanced understanding of etiquette have to learn new skills. For example, with increasing use of on-screen technology and remote working, it is important to understand how to project a confident and assertive on-screen persona.

As business becomes increasingly international and society becomes more sensitive to issues of respect, equality and non-discrimination, it is ever more important for employers to understand, and effectively manage, the workplace culture they create. Workplaces where staff are considerate and attuned to each other are happy and productive; employees are loyal and less likely to move on. Customers and clients will evaluate a company by looking at the demeanour of its staff: employees who are polite, friendly, respectful and courteous will always be an asset to an employer.

FOREWORD

Workplaces which are more diverse and accepting, both ethnically and culturally, outperform those which are not, making it increasingly important for companies to create an inclusive culture in which talent from all diversities can thrive. Diversity increases employee satisfaction, helps to retain existing employees and attracts new staff, reduces recruitment costs and increases productivity. It helps companies to better represent the communities they serve and understand how their customers think and what drives their spending habits. This in turn helps them access markets that they had not previously been able to tap into so effectively.

One the best teachers I had the privilege to study under at Harvard Business School was Professor Frances X. Frei. Professor Frei delivered a virtual lecture during the pandemic explaining trust as a triangle; to engender trust she says you need to have authenticity, logic, and empathy. Empathy and good manners go hand in hand, because you are not just thinking of yourself, but you are thinking of others – it is not what is in it for me; it is what is in it for you.

Good manners go hand in hand with an attitude not of being the best in the world, but for the world, and good leaders have good manners. The true test of leadership is not in the good times but in times of adversity. My late father, Lieutenant General Faridoon Noshir Bilimoria, who was in command of a battalion of 350,000 troops in times of war, always said you had to be cool, calm and collected during a crisis. It is during these occasions that good manners win the day by encouraging the confidence and trust of the people whom you are leading. Good leaders, good manners and decorum are time tested and timeless.

Lord Bilimoria of Chelsea CBE, DL

CHAPTER 01

OFFICE WORKING & HOME WORKING

What is an Office?

An office is not a social gathering of friends. It is a place that has to have rules and procedures and practices that are clearly known to all who work there; and the bigger it is, the more people it employs, the more difficult it is to establish unanimity of thought about such rules and procedures. This is why the smooth running of any such office is enormously helped by the occupants understanding and practising good business etiquette.

1. An office is a place where a number of people come together to work for a common purpose.

2. It has a hierarchy, however gently that structure sits upon the office.

3. Most people are attending the office mainly (if not entirely) because they are paid to do so.

4. Very few of them have any say in who else is employed in that office.

An office is a place where we are judged – by our juniors, our peers and our bosses. If we do well, if we fit in, if we become prized members of staff, we may look forward to promotion.

If we do not fit in comfortably with office culture, then we may be the first to go when cuts have to be made. We may be great at our job, but we have also to be decent, civilised, polite human beings, producing office-appropriate behaviour at our place of work.

Pre-eminently, this is a place where there are seniors and juniors, employers and employees, those who make the rules and those who have to follow them. It doesn't take much for things to go very wrong. A manager's thoughtless or high-handed remark can result in a previously conscientious worker deciding that he or she is never again going to put the company first. A failure to greet a visitor promptly with due politeness will tarnish the company's image – perhaps with disastrous results. Once things start going wrong, they have a habit of getting worse. Every institution can become a breeding place for bad feelings, can develop a bad atmosphere, and its employees can slip into bad habits.

Some institutions try to limit damage by having elaborate systems of rules covering behaviour. Few offices go this far, but most rely on an unwritten code of conduct – and mutual understanding as to how we should behave towards each other. This is the foundation of business etiquette.

THE BEST
WAY TO
APPRECIATE
YOUR JOB IS
TO IMAGINE
YOURSELF
WITHOUT
ONE.

Oscar Wilde

Physical Office Space

Offices were traditionally physical spaces that were minutely calibrated on hierarchical principles. The higher-status workers were allocated their own offices, with doors that could be shut, walls that were opaque and even, if they were lucky, windows with views of the outside world. Lower-status workers were relegated to a communal space, possibly with some degree of internal division to create semi-private cubicles. Privacy was thus a higher status privilege, easily attainable by those who had their own offices, not afforded to the workers in the communal areas.

In the twenty-first century, office spaces have become much more fluid, and in some cases, more democratic. Managers may share the same physical space as their team members, without any obvious tangible division. In some offices, desks are not even assigned; the practice of 'hot desking' means that employees select and use desks on an ad hoc basis.

It is theorised that, if employees work together in a shared open-plan space, they will be able to behave spontaneously; asking colleagues questions, convening impromptu meetings, picking up on other strands of the business and how it is conducted.

However, a shared workspace offers no privacy. Every conversation is subject to eavesdropping, and distractions are endless. A solution is to provide a number of 'break-out' meeting rooms, but workers will be aware that withdrawing to these rooms with other colleagues sends out a strong message about asserting privacy, and will certainly indicate that confidential information is being discussed.

There are many offices that fall between these two ends of the spectrum, and a number of factors will be taken into account when planning office space:

- Is the office hierarchical and is status important?

- Do your employees work in small, discrete teams? (the arrangement of their desks should reflect this).

- Is privacy a strong requisite for some employees/roles?

- Do you feel the business will benefit from the creativity and buzz of a communal atmosphere, or will it simply create noise and distraction?

See Privacy in the Office pp 92–97

Hot Desking

The practice of 'hot desking', when desks are not assigned to individual employees and are allocated on a first-come, first-served basis has evolved because it gives managers a great deal of flexibility when it comes to allocating their office space.

However, before you decide to introduce this system, be aware that there are a number of disadvantages:

1. Employees who are not assigned their own desk, and hence their own territory, may feel undervalued.

2. Many employees will feel that, without a permanent base in the office, they may just as well be working from home.

3. If hot desking is introduced in a very large company, employees can disappear from view, and become inaccessible.

4. Because hot desking creates random seating arrangements, the likelihood is that employees will not be seated next to colleagues with whom they are working or collaborating. They will not be able to have impromptu meetings, or simply exchange information.

5. Seeking help from fellow employees may involve long walks around the office, or protracted email exchanges. These are time-wasting distractions.

If your company has a very limited number of employees, then a small office becomes a useful communal space, and loosely-structured seating is not a disadvantage.

Hot Desk Syndrome

If you find yourself assigned a hot desk, a little bit of consideration will make the experience more tolerable for those that follow you. Nobody wants to become a notorious abuser of the hot desk syndrome:

- Leave everything as you found it – eg put the chair back under the desk, line up the computer so that it faces the chair etc.

- If you are sharing a computer as well as a desk, do your successor the courtesy of giving the computer keyboard and screen a quick wipe.

- Similarly, ensure that you have not left coffee mug rings or food debris in any nooks and crannies that might be overlooked by cleaners.

- Ensure that all your personal possessions have been removed.

- Before leaving, check to make sure that you haven't taken vital supplies (eg pens and post-it notes) with you.

Home Working

The days of a rigid adherence to the 9–5 working day, and a career that spanned an entire adult life and ended with retirement, are long gone. While some of us choose the more conventional institutions of working life, opting for security, predictability and certainty, many of us are now taking a more adventurous and haphazard journey. This may be because of our own personalities, or the nature of our work, but it could also be because many employers are operating new practices, and relying less on permanent staff members and more on consultants, freelance employees, part-time workers, job-sharers, or people who are working on zero-hours contracts.

This change in working practices has led to an increased acceptance of home working. Mobile phones and WiFi have expedited the change, meaning that employees are available (sometimes 24/7), communication is easy, and video calls and conferencing can be deployed to maintain contact. Some home workers mix and match their working styles; for example, basing themselves mainly at home but consenting to attend an office once a week for meetings and consultancy.

Is Home Working Right for Me?

While working from home has many advantages, both for the employer and employee, there are several factors to be taken into consideration. If you are an employer who is thinking about making home working available for your employees, you must be aware that this will inevitably involve forfeiting a degree of control, and trusting your employees to fulfil their responsibilities without being constantly monitored.

Employers should consider the following:

1. Do you trust your employees to use their time constructively?

2. If you feel you need to closely monitor your employees' activity and output when working from home, you may find that administrative oversight is too burdensome.

3. Do you thrive on interaction with employees, and enjoy stimulating ad hoc conversations in the office? If so, you might prefer to keep them in-house.

4. Are you able to compartmentalise working life, perhaps meeting employees just once a week for a detailed catch-up? If so, you will probably be happy to let them work from home.

5. Are you a demanding employer who expects employees to be readily available and accessible? If so, home working might not suit your management style – while you may be able to reach home workers on their mobiles, that will not necessarily mean that they are available to meet your demands.

6. Are you willing to support home workers? Perhaps you would be prepared to supply an ergonomic office chair? Or you might be amenable to covering expenses like broadband and electricity.

> Out of clutter, find simplicity.
> From discord, find harmony. In the
> middle of difficulty lies opportunity
> Albert Einstein

If you are thinking of working from home, bear in mind the following:

- Do you have sufficient space at home in which to work? Ideally, you would have a dedicated room; if you are forced to work from your sofa, bed or dining table, home working might not be for you.

- Are you an extrovert, who thrives on social contact, and loves chatting by the water cooler or coffee machine? Home working can be lonely.

- Are you disciplined and organised? To work effectively from home you will need to be a self-starter, who can make clear distinctions between home life and working life.

- Are you a night owl or an early bird, who functions best at these times? If so, home working might well be ideal for you, as to a certain extent you can call the shots and work at the times that best suit you.

- Do you have complicated childcare arrangements, or perhaps responsibility for an elderly parent? These responsibilities can be very difficult to integrate into conventional working life, but home-based working gives you the autonomy and flexibility you need.

- Do you have plenty of social contacts outside work? You will need to ensure that you have an active social life to compensate for the hours you spend working alone.

- When the right conditions are met, home working can be highly effective. It gives employees flexibility and independence, and they may find themselves much more efficient and productive in a quiet home study than in a noisy office.

A MAN WHO DARES TO WASTE ONE HOUR OF LIFE HAS NOT DISCOVERED THE VALUE OF LIFE.

CHARLES DARWIN

The Home Office

If you are sure that you can run a home working operation on a laptop balanced on your knees while you're lounging on your bed, think again. You need to think seriously about a dedicated workspace, no matter how modest, where you can shut a door, leave out papers and files, hold private conversations. You will also need to ensure that the rest of your household, or family, understand and respect these parameters.

What you need in your home office at the bare minimum:

- A desk, or sturdy table.

- A chair, preferably an ergonomic office chair, to ensure you don't end up with back problems.

- An anglepoise light, which will help you to avoid eye strain.

- A shelf, or drawer in which you can store papers or files.

- Most importantly of all, a reliable WiFi connection, which works in your office (if your hub is several rooms away, and especially if your house has thick walls, invest in a signal booster).

Remember that, in these days of video calls, you may well be observed in your home office, so ensure that you have an acceptable backdrop. A bare wall is the safest choice of all, although your colleagues may find it depressingly bland. If you have bookshelves, ensure that they are neat and tidy. Try to avoid too much personal clutter, such as photographs and ornaments – the people you work with will be distracted by your possessions, and will enjoy speculating about what they say about your private life.

CHAPTER 02

Job Applications

Most people make their entry into an office after the baptism of fire known as the job application and interview.

The first hurdle is to complete a job application, comprising a covering letter and CV, which are sufficiently attention-grabbing and professional to secure you an interview. Alternatively you might be required to fill in an online application, completing questions about your education and career, submitting a personal statement and uploading your CV.

The interview is a long-standing custom that recently has been refined and extended, and nowadays potential candidates may be subjected to a day or more of meetings and tours around the office and tests of physical, mental and moral aptitude. In some cases, interviews will be no more than a casual and relaxed chat over a cup of coffee – bear in mind that the nature of the interview will tell you a great deal about the company culture.

Covering Letters and CVs

These documents should be clearly laid out, legible and professional looking. Avoid typefaces that mimic handwriting, or jaunty, joking typefaces like Comic Sans. Opt instead for something classic and elegant – a safe default is Times Roman.

Ensure that both these documents have a legible header that clearly displays your name, address, phone number and email. No employer is going to waste time scrabbling around trying to find ways in which to contact you.

Finally, both of these documents need to be thoroughly checked. The top three things that turn off employers are bad grammar, spelling mistakes and poor formatting. Take advantage of simple online templates or even use your own creativity – just remember to have a fresh pair of eyes look at your CV before you send it.

Compiling Your Curriculum Vitae

Of course you will want to show yourself off in the best light, but be careful about exaggerating and making claims about your career that you will not be able to substantiate when questioned.

There are myriad ways in which you can choose to present your CV. Your choice should reflect the stage which you have reached in your career, and which aspects of it you want to bring to the foreground. If your career progression has been steady and uncontroversial, you will probably choose to present your working life chronologically. If, on the other hand, you have had many jobs and there are unexplained gaps and absences, it might be more sensible to go for a skills-based CV, which reflects on your various attributes and specialisms, and how you acquired them.

In general, CVs start with your education, and your job history (if you are taking the chronological approach) is listed with your most recent employer first. Don't use long paragraphs – it's hard work for employers and will put them off. It is really helpful to spell out exactly what skills you acquired and utilised in previous jobs.

Bullet points will break up the text and make it easy to read. You do not have to present your entire life story – edit the information, keep it short, concise and relevant.

Listing hobbies such as 'socialising with friends and going to the gym' will sell you short. They don't demonstrate what value you're bringing to the company. Only include hobbies that will have a positive spin, eg running marathons (striving to push yourself to the limits), playing in the local football team (team player), amateur theatricals (creative people person etc).

Don't be afraid to include details of your social media accounts (eg Twitter, LinkedIn, blogs) but only do this if you think they are a positive reflection of you. It's becoming more common for employers to search for potential employees online, so by including this information you are making it easier for them to find you.

Finally, review your CV every time you apply for a new job. Advertisements will highlight the key skills that are required, and you must present your experience in a way that will demonstrate that you possess these skills. This might mean tweaking and editing your CV to reflect specific requirements.

Sending Your CV

Most CVs are now sent digitally, so avoid sending large files with system-slowing attachments. If you are applying for a job where you want to include a portfolio, ask if the employer would like to see your work and then send it separately through a file transfer protocol.

Don't use obscure software to create your CV. Microsoft Word is universally used in the world of work. Alternatively you can save your CV as a pdf, another universal medium.

You will need to provide the details of referees at the end of your CV (two are sufficient), or you can add the phrase 'References on request'. If you are citing referees by name, it is a basic courtesy to secure their agreement in principle to your request.

Your Covering Letter

It is increasingly unlikely that you will send a covering letter in the post, since most job applications are now digital. Nevertheless, it is recommended that you treat this communication as essentially a letter in digital form.

If the job advertisement calls for a CV and covering letter, then you should probably format the letter in the conventional way and send it as a Word attachment, with a very brief email accompanying your application, just stating the position that you are seeking. If this is not specified, then it is quite acceptable to treat your email as the covering letter.

This vital document is the first thing any potential employer will read, and it will determine whether they actually look at your CV or not.

> Our goals can only be reached through the vehicle of a plan, in which we must fervently believe, and upon which we must vigorously act. There is no other route to success.
>
> Pablo Picasso

To ensure that your letter acts as an excellent, and enticing, introduction to your application, follow these rules:

1. It should be no longer than an A4 page. If you are required to apply by post, it should be printed on good quality paper (white or cream, not coloured).

2. Try your utmost to personalise the letter, using the name of the person to whom you're writing, and the correct title (Mr, Mrs, Miss, Ms). This may involve making a telephone enquiry before sending off your application. Only use 'Dear Sir or Madam' if you have no other option.

3. Add a subject line to the letter (underneath the 'Dear…'). This could be the job title, or the reference number given in the job advertisement.

4. Check the letter forensically for the correct use of spelling and grammar.

5. If the advertisement calls for a handwritten covering letter (which happens occasionally), it is a clear indication that your application should be sent by post.

6. Indicate in the letter that you know about the organisation you are applying to. Research the company before you write the letter, and perhaps refer to the fact that you have visited the company website.

7. Explain, briefly, why you are interested in the specific job, and why you think you are a suitable applicant.

8. If you are replying to an advertisement that calls for specific skills, experience or qualifications, you must make it clear that you meet these requirements.

If you are sending your application by post, attach your covering letter to your CV with a paper clip and send them in a good quality envelope that matches the stationery you have used. A well-presented job application will be let down by a utilitarian brown envelope.

CHOOSE A JOB YOU LOVE, AND YOU WILL NEVER HAVE TO WORK A DAY IN YOUR LIFE.

CONFUCIUS

Interviews

The purpose of a job interview, and the form that it takes, is to discover whether or not the candidate is the right person for the job. This involves examining how well the candidate will fit in with current office staff and practice.

At its best, the interview is a two-way process. Both sides are on trial. In a highly competitive job market it may be that the interviewee has the most to lose, but that shouldn't mean that those conducting the interview can behave in a high-handed fashion. Any employer wants the best possible recruit to the staff. It would be a grave mistake to have the ideal applicant turn down a job because the interviewers were rude or thoughtless.

Conducting an Interview

Thought should always be given as to how an interview is to be conducted. There are a lot of questions that need to be answered. If it is a formal interview, how many people should be on the 'panel'? Who should be in charge? How long should the interview last? How should the seating be arranged? How should each candidate be greeted? What time should be allotted for candidates to ask their own questions?

Most offices have long established their own procedures, but it doesn't hurt to run a regular checklist over the tried, and possibly tired, formula. And it shouldn't be necessary to remind those holding an interview that, if it has to be cancelled or postponed for any reason, the candidate should be told as soon as possible.

Some indication as to the size and make-up of the interviewing panel or the parameters of the interview should have been already communicated to the candidate by phone or letter.

> They always say time changes things, but you actually have to change them yourself.
> Andy Warhol

Where Should the Interview Take Place?

If only one person is conducting the interview, then there is no question about who is in charge. But thought needs to be given to where the interview should take place, and how the seating should be arranged. The interview room should be clean, tidy and businesslike, giving the sort of impression that the company wishes to project.

It's not a good idea to interview someone in a corridor or on a couple of chairs in the corner of the reception area. It suggests that the interview is a nuisance, a half forgotten piece of trivia that's getting in the way of what really matters. On the other hand, an interview conducted in a conference chamber the size of the concourse at Paddington station is hardly likely to put the candidate at ease and allow him or her to give of their best.

If it's a one-to-one interview, then preferably it should take place in the interviewer's own office, probably with the two parties sitting on opposite sides of the desk, though some prefer a more side-by-side approach.

If the candidate is to be interviewed by a panel, then the choice is an open one. Some prefer the panel to sit behind a table or tables (arranged in an inverted U-shape if there are lots of people interviewing); others prefer a circle of chairs. It isn't fair, and it's bad manners, to make candidates face interviewers who are sitting with their backs to windows or other sources of light, so that all the candidate sees is a series of silhouettes. Not only is it bad manners, it's inefficient because it prevents candidates performing to the best of their abilities, and the company may therefore turn down someone they should have taken.

Asking Questions

At the appointed hour for the interview, the chair of the interviewing panel, or the individual interviewer, should open proceedings by introducing himself/herself, ushering the candidate into the interview room, and showing them where to sit. He/she should start by making the candidate feel welcome, asking if he or she has had a good journey, thanking them for coming, and saying how pleased the company is to meet them. The next thing is to outline how the interview will be conducted, what its purpose is, roughly how long it will last, and what time will be set aside for the candidate to ask questions of the panel or interviewer.

The next order of priority is to make the necessary introductions if there is an interview panel. This should be done slowly and deliberately because it takes a long time to register who's who. After this the questions can begin.

Acceptable Topics

It is fair enough to ask candidates questions about their previous work record and experience, about any problems they might have travelling to the job, about their career ambitions, etc. It is not acceptable to ask questions about their political allegiances, religious beliefs, or plans to start a family. If candidates are asked such questions, they have to edge their ways diplomatically around them, but those asking such questions lose a great many points and may well be breaking the law.

The ways in which questions are asked will set the whole tone of the interview. If the questions are too forceful, then there is the danger that the interview will quickly become confrontational. If they're not forceful enough, little will be discovered about the candidates. Good interview questions are open ended, they will allow the candidates chances to speak at some length. 'Do you think you would be good at this job?' is not as helpful a question as 'how are you suited to this job?' It doesn't elicit information, it doesn't draw the candidate out, it doesn't invite a whole spectrum of answers from a range of candidates – and that's what is needed for the panel to make a decision.

Offering Refreshments

Refreshments can pose problems at interviews. If coffee or tea is served halfway through the interview, it breaks the flow of the meeting. If it's served at the end, the whole thing becomes an uncomfortable tea party. Better to give the candidate a cup of tea or coffee on arrival, preferably while they're waiting, so that they can get it out of their way. Nobody is at their best balancing a cup on their knee, munching a biscuit and trying to answer questions intelligently at the same time.

Concluding the Interview

At the end of the interview, the candidates should be asked if there are any questions they wish to ask. When it is clear that these have been dealt with, the interview should be brought to an end by the chairperson. Each candidate is again thanked for attending, and it should be made clear when and how they will be informed of the outcome of the application.

The chairperson or whoever conducted the interview should write to all candidates after a decision has been made, or earlier if that decision is likely to be delayed. It's extremely bad manners to leave candidates to assume that they haven't got the job simply because they haven't heard anything and several weeks have passed.

How the Interviewee Should Behave

1. The first thing for any candidate to do is to respond to the invitation to the interview – ie to let the recruiter know whether or not he or she will attend. Candidates should research the company before attending interviews: a lot of information can be gleaned from websites, especially the 'About us' section.

2. The next priority is to present yourself to your best advantage. Obviously you should never turn up looking crumpled or ill-dressed. Given the great range of office environments in the 21st century, it might be wise to do some research before the interview to ensure that you are 'reading' the company correctly. Wearing a city-smart suit (and tie for men), with polished shoes or your best heels, to an interview at a company where everyone wears jeans, sweatshirts and trainers might seem uncomfortably anomalous. While you may not want to completely mirror the super-casual style, it might be wise to downplay your clothes and go for something more understated.

3. On the day of the interview it is vital to arrive at the right place at the right time. Research the route to the office and the public transport options before your interview day. The trouble is that trains are often late, roads are often blocked, buses don't materialise – so none of these excuses is impressive and none of them brings any real sympathy. Simply having recourse to your mobile and texting a message that you've been delayed wins points for communication but the fact that you haven't been able to arrive at the interview on time may well count against you. Many people are increasingly frustrated that text updates are being used as a substitute for punctuality.

4. If something disastrous happens, something way beyond your control, and you know you are going to be late, then you should communicate this information as soon and as politely as possible.

5. When you arrive at the interview you should take notice of who and what is around you. Smiling at the receptionist, doorman, and any staff who greet you always helps. You might leave a favourable impression with a colleague of your interviewer, which will help your case.

6. It's wise to assume that you should adopt the tone of the panel or interviewer. Be wary of over-familiarity – it might be a test. It's best to be polite, but not ingratiatingly so. Nerves may well be apparent – in extremis you can always acknowledge that you are feeling nervous.

7. Questions should be answered as directly as possible – experienced panels and interviewers have a built-in radar for recognising waffle. If you don't understand the question, say so, and ask for it to be repeated, or rephrased or explained. Take your time. A deliberate pause when you are asked a question will not be detrimental – it shows that you are thinking about your answer.

8. Save your own questions for the end of the interview unless invited to state them earlier. It's quite permissible to ask about the salary, conditions of employment, whether there is a staff canteen etc. It isn't a good idea to ask if you can have the first two weeks off in June before you've even been offered the job. When it's clear that the interview is over, thank the panel generally, and the chairperson in particular, or the sole interviewer, and then take your leave.

9. If they don't tell you when and how you will hear the results of the interview, it does no harm to ask.

After the Interview

It is acceptable to write a follow-up letter after or email the interview, thanking the chair of the interview panel (or your individual interviewer) for their time and hospitality. But you should take great care not to make such a letter seem sycophantic.

If you are offered the job (and still want it), write to accept at once – this is the business world we are dealing with, and no points will be gained by showing restraint or trying to suggest that you are so busy that you've hardly time to acknowledge their important communication.

If you didn't get the job, it is permissible to write or email (not phone) and ask if you could be given reasons why you didn't succeed. You may not like the reply, but there's no harm in asking. No company has to justify its decision in giving a job to one candidate rather than another, but it isn't unreasonable for the successful candidate to want to know what went wrong with their own application. Once you've been given that reason, the matter is closed.

I SPEAK TWO LANGUAGES: BODY AND ENGLISH.

Mae West

Body language for Interviews

When you walk into an interview you should proffer your hand on being introduced. A firm handshake should last no more than a few seconds. Use your right hand, ensure that your fingers grip the other person's palm and 'pump' the hand two or three times before you let it go. Check your palms are not sweaty or clammy before shaking hands.

It matters how you sit, what you do with your legs and arms and hands, and even how you walk into an interview. An upright posture looks alert and businesslike. Crossed arms indicate a defensive attitude. Hands in pockets, be it trousers or jackets, will look over-nonchalant, or even arrogant. Legs may be crossed, but not ostentatiously so, and not if such an action reveals a stretch of flesh above the sock top or too much leg.

Maintain steady eye contact throughout the interview. This does not mean staring fixedly at your questioner; it is acceptable to intermittently look away. Don't become so obsessed with maintaining eye contact that you actually forget to focus on the conversation. Remember to smile when appropriate; it will communicate warmth and establish trust.

The face should be left alone during the interview. Picking at your teeth or nose, or fussing with your hairstyle will lose points. If you have to blow your nose, there is no harm in that, so don't try to do it furtively.

The hands should be as still as possible, though it's quite acceptable to gesticulate to add emphasis to what you are saying. What has to be avoided is waving them about, or fidgeting with your fingers, nails or cuticles. This can be distracting for the interviewers and interferes with their concentration on what you are saying. In extreme cases it may make them think that they are dealing with someone who is clearly neurotic.

If you are really uncomfortable, then say so. Maybe there is something wrong with the chair, or you're suddenly feeling ill. It's better to ask for another hearing or a break in the proceedings if you feel you are performing way below your potential or because you are not well.

Video Interviews

Increasingly, many of our important transactions are taking place online, including the all-important job interview. There are several potential traps and pitfalls, but with a little thought and advance planning, and a few tricks, you should be able to conquer the medium and show yourself off at your best.

Before the Interview

- Practice makes perfect. If you feel discomfited by the digital medium and are convinced that it does not do you any favours, enlist a patient friend to conduct some mock interviews beforehand. Elicit an honest response and you will learn how to maximise your online impact.

- Test and test again. Technical glitches are a pointless and irritating distraction, so test your equipment beforehand and ensure that your microphone is working and that your camera is in the right position – remember to try and level the lens with your eyes, not your chin, or you will look jowly and distorted.

- Indulge in a little set-dressing. Evaluate your image on the screen and assess what is visible in the background. Try and go for as neutral a backdrop as possible; zany photographs, quirky memorabilia, provocative posters, chaotic bookshelves or discarded items of clothing will not make you look interesting and original, they will be an irritating distraction for the interviewer, who might also conclude that your clutter indicates a disorganised mind.

- Tidy your space. Even if the room in which you're doing your interview isn't visible on-screen, spruce it up and clear away extraneous clutter. This is important because it will focus your mind, reminding you that you're not slumped in front of your computer casually chatting to a friend, you're engaged in a professional, and challenging, interchange.

- Warn your household. Make sure that everyone is aware that your room is off-bounds and that you must not be interrupted. You might even want to stick a notice on your door. Impress on your housemates, partner or family that loud shouting or pounding music may actually be audible. Be very careful around small children, who will blithely ignore verbal warnings, and ensure that they are being closely monitored, or preferably taken out, and kept a safe distance from the house.

- Beware digital interruptions. It goes without saying that you should mute your phone before the interview, but also be aware that open and running apps and programmes on your computer may disgorge a noisy series of tones and pings that could be an irritating distraction.

- Dress for success. You will obviously need to look smart and well-groomed and, while an online interview may not call for sharp tailoring, it is important that you look well turned-out. Avoid dressing from head to foot in black as it will look overwhelmingly sober, and avoid white as it may 'blind' the viewer. Remember that stripes and other patterns can create a shimmering effect on screen, which can be very distracting. Dress as if you can be seen from top-to-toe; it's true the interviewer will not be able to see your joggers or pyjama bottoms, but baggy comfortable clothes may create a dangerous feeling of relaxation. Your smart clothes will remind you what is at stake and why you are there.

ON-SCREEN ETIQUETTE

- Follow good on-screen protocols. It's important to maintain eye contact and not to be distracted by your own image in the corner of the screen. Try to use your face to convey expressions, and avoid expansive hand gestures. When you are listening to your interviewer, sit still, don't fidget and avoid fiddling with your face, beard or hair. Sit up straight, with your shoulders back and your feet planted firmly on the floor. You can lean into the screen for emphasis, but don't lean back in your chair.

- Beware interrupting and talking-over. When the interviewer asks you a question, nod to show that you are listening, but pause briefly before starting on your answer. This will ensure that you do not interrupt or talk over the interviewer. The small hiatuses that result are much more acceptable than interruptions, and, as long as you look engaged and focused, will not be detrimental.

CHAPTER 03
INTRODUCTIONS

Inevitably, office life involves meeting new people – be they colleagues, clients or customers. It is important, especially in a business context, to understand how to make clear and polite introductions, so that names are registered, and roles are noted.

The point at which introductions are made is the moment when people make the most impact on each other. So enunciating names clearly, engaging in eye contact, smiling, and offering a firm handshake, are all vital tools when it comes to making a good impression.

Handshakes

A handshake is now the almost universal method of greeting, especially in business or formal situations. It is the correct way to greet colleagues, clients, customers, diplomats, dignitaries.

A firm handshake, lasting a few seconds, is the common form of greeting for all business situations and most social situations too. Always use your right hand, and 'pump' the hand two or three times before you let it go. Ensure that your fingers grip the other person's palm, otherwise you will crush their fingers. Be careful not to clench the other person's hand in a bone-crushing grip, but do not offer a limp hand. Check that your palms are not sweaty or clammy before shaking hands.

Use your right hand, and do not bring the left hand down on top of the entwined right hands to indicate sincerity.

Be aware that in some situations, a handshake is not appropriate. Muslims do not shake hands with members of the opposite sex; instead, the man will place his hand, palm down, just above his heart and slightly bow his head in greeting.

Bowing is the traditional form of greeting in many East Asian countries, but handshakes are widely used and accepted, especially in business scenarios.

> **You can't stay in your corner of the forest waiting for others to come to you. You have to go to them sometimes.**
> A.A. Milne

EVERYONE YOU MEET KNOWS SOMETHING YOU DON'T KNOW BUT NEED TO KNOW. LEARN FROM THEM.

C.G. JUNG

Greeting with a Kiss

Within the framework of business etiquette, the general rule is don't. Of course, if a client or colleague is also a friend, that's a different matter, but otherwise it should never be assumed that even a gentle kiss is acceptable. Like all general rules, this has exceptions, the most obvious being when in certain foreign countries, for example France, and in certain industries, such as fashion and PR.

If you find yourself in a business situation where a kiss is proffered, don't look taken aback. Usually your right cheek is offered first and you should briefly touch cheeks. You will need to read the body language of the person who is greeting you to establish if you are being offered a double, or even triple, kiss. Customs vary, so remain poised to comply.

How to Introduce People

In the past, office hierarchies were reinforced by forms of address: bosses and people who were higher up in the pecking order were always referred to as 'Mr', 'Mrs', or 'Ms'. More junior staff were referred to by their forename – an effective way of putting everyone in their place. Increasingly, British life has become much less formal, and forenames are the order of the day.

If you are the link between people who have never met, it is up to you to make the introductions. In the business (as in the social) context, an introduction can be a way of conveying a useful nugget of information about the people who are being introduced – their job title, or a brief summary of their role. It can certainly be useful in a work context to provide surnames:

1. Introduce juniors to seniors ('Paul, may I introduce Bill Dorsey? Paul Goodman is our senior vice president. Bill is one of our part-time researchers').

2. Introduce men to women ('Sandra, this is Robert Shaw, our staff liaison officer. Sandra Day is Max Herman's new personal assistant').

3. Introduce colleagues to clients ('James, I'd like you to meet Mark Bassey. Mark heads up our UK sales team. Mark, James Alsop is the chief buyer at PNG Enterprises').

When you are gathering together for a meeting, introduce individuals to the group first and then the group to the individual. For example, 'Clare, this is James, Daniel and Anna. Everyone, this is Clare'. You can gesture, or nod, towards the relevant person to add clarity. Unless the occasion is formal there's no need to mention surnames, and with long lists of names it can become too cumbersome. If possible, offering a little information about each person as you introduce them ('Daniel and I were on the graduate training scheme together') will help to break the ice. These extra details are also a good way of fixing names and faces in the memory.

Traditionally, when introduced, a handshake is followed by the formal greeting 'How do you do?', to which the correct response is 'How do you do?'. This question does not mean 'How are you?'.

In informal situations, however, the standard response to an introduction is a friendly 'Hello, good to meet you'.

The Formal Way

There may be instances when full formality is required – perhaps if you and your colleagues are being introduced to a visiting dignitary or a titled person, or the CEO of your company. Or you might be making introductions to an older person, who is not accustomed to the less formal manners we all use today. You will have to utilise your social antennae to assess when these rare circumstances arise.

If you are seeking to introduce an element of old-fashioned formality, it is signalled by a refusal to rely on forenames, and a tendency to use titles such as 'Mr', 'Mrs' and 'Ms'. However, it would be rare for this level of formality to exist in most British offices.

- 'Mr Goodman, may I introduce Tommy Dorsey? Mr Goodman is our senior vice president. Tommy is one of our part-time researchers.'
- 'Ms Day, this is Mr Shaw, our staff liaison officer. Ms Day is Mr Herman's new personal assistant.'
- 'Mr Alsop, I'd like you to meet Mr Bassey. Mark Bassey heads up our UK sales team. Mark, James Alsop is the chief buyer at PNG Enterprises.'

If you are introducing people, there is no need to wave your hands expansively to and fro during this process, but most people do. Grabbing those being introduced by the wrist or shoulder in an effort to bring them physically closer to each other is not a good idea.

What matters far more than theatrical gestures is that the verbal introductions are delivered in a clear voice and at a reasonable speed. The aim of the whole process is to enable strangers to learn each other's names and roles.

Forgetting Names

Remembering the names of people to whom you have been introduced can be a haphazard business. Some names are unusual or memorable, and will therefore stick in your mind. Others are instantly forgettable, and drastic measures need to be taken.

Using the name a couple of times in conversation soon after you've first heard it might fix it in your memory (but don't overdo this, or you'll sound like an importunate salesman).

Try visualisation techniques. For example, as soon as you hear the name, mentally blazon it across the person's forehead.

Or try a mnemonic; think of something memorable that rhymes with the name. Don't become so obsessed with remembering the name that you fail to participate in the conversation, however.

If you do forget, don't panic – you can generally negotiate your way through a conversation without naming names, and you can always find out later. If all else fails, a charming and self-deprecating 'I'm so sorry, I'm terrible at remembering names, I always do this …' should ensure that your memory lapse doesn't offend anyone.

On being introduced, it is quite permissible to ask for a name or title to be repeated, and even, if it's a complicated or unusual name that you still haven't grasped, to ask for it to be spelt out. It is far better to show a genuine desire to get someone's name right and learn it than to act as though it isn't worth committing to memory.

VIPs

It doesn't happen all the time, but it is not unknown in the business world to come across ambassadors, princes, ministers or aristocrats. There are more complex rules about how to introduce special people – those of rank or official standing. For correct forms of address please refer to specialist reference sources, such as Debrett's *Handbook*.

Business Card Etiquette

When you are introduced in a business context (for example at a client meeting, networking event or sales conference), it may be appropriate to present your business card. Be discerning about handing out business cards – papering a room with them will look somewhat desperate.

Always hand a business card to the recipient with your right hand, with the text facing uppermost so it is immediately legible.

Make sure that your cards are easily accessible – scrabbling around for a business card in the bottom of your bag or your pockets does not look very professional.

Store business cards in a card holder to ensure they are in pristine condition, or keep half a dozen business cards in your wallet or credit card holder.

If you are handed a business card, try and make a polite comment about it. You could say something complimentary about the logo or the design, or comment on the location of head office. This will demonstrate that you have noted the card and value it.

Avoid handing out business cards on social occasions. If you would like to take a social acquaintance further in a business context, ask your hostess for an introduction.

DO I NOT DESTROY MY ENEMIES WHEN I MAKE THEM MY FRIENDS?

Abraham Lincoln

OFFICE MANNERS

CHAPTER 04

People feel they are appreciated when they are treated with politeness. When people feel at ease with each other, and there is mutual respect, the office culture will be happy and productive.

There are certain cardinal rules about working in an office that will go some way towards fostering team spirit:

1. Don't use other people's desks as temporary (or permanent) dumping grounds for files, folders, newspapers, empty coffee mugs and sandwiches.

2. Observe the social pleasantries: a friendly 'Good morning' will buy infinitely more good will than a Neanderthal grunt.

3. Don't lean over to a neighbouring desk to pinch pens, envelopes, sticky labels or a stapler when there aren't any on your own.

4. Don't expect someone else always to make the tea, water the plants, put new toilet rolls in the staff loos, or wash the mugs.

5. Don't always expect someone else to answer the phone at an unoccupied desk. If you do answer the unattended phone, leave a legible, and coherent, message.

6. Listen politely to ongoing conversations in the office and don't cut across them because you think you've got something important to say.

7. Don't calibrate your behaviour according to office hierarchies, treating the office manager with obsequious civility and behaving arrogantly towards junior assistants.

8. Don't assume just because you're employed as a manager that it would be wrong to open the door for a colleague, or help to carry boxes of stationery across the room.

IT IS AMAZING
WHAT
YOU CAN
ACCOMPLISH
IF YOU DO
NOT CARE
WHO GETS
THE CREDIT.

Harry S Truman

Valuing the Office Culture

Building teams, working cooperatively, and appreciating and acknowledging your colleagues are the foundation stones of the office culture. This is constructed from a myriad of small actions, from taking it in turns to do the office tea round to sharing praise at the end of a big project.

Establishing these codes of conduct and helping to implement them should be the responsibility of someone on the office staff. Whether an office is a pleasant or disagreeable place to work depends on everyone in it. In that way, it is a true democracy.

Team Work

Most offices work on the premise that the staff constitutes a team. But this important fact is often ignored.

Nothing undermines a team more than the tendency not to share credit when something is going right, which is of course matched by a tendency to blame others when things go wrong.

Functioning teams will always be appreciative of the demands being made on their members. Quite frequently a subordinate will have to reschedule all his or her work to meet the demands of a senior. The logistics may be unavoidable; the assumption that the assistant needs no special thanks or appreciation is entirely avoidable.

For a team to work well everyone needs to be broadly aware of what everyone else is doing. Regular team meetings are a way of keeping colleagues appraised of ongoing projects, deadlines, and crises. This means that, in extremis, colleagues are ready and available to step in and help fellow team members when things go wrong or become pressurised.

It is generally a sign that a team is not cohering when people keep very quiet when volunteers are called for to contribute to a work effort or even to organise a social occasion.

Pretty speeches and mass emails have limited effectiveness in assembling a team. Personal example is what is needed.

Building a Team

Remember that the most effective team leaders bring their members together by fostering an atmosphere of trust and loyalty. Threats, tantrums and meltdowns may bring short-term productivity, but ultimately will annihilate any spirit of good will and cooperation.

1. Display good manners at all times – opening doors for those with a handful, whoever they may be; holding the lift doors open for those who would otherwise just miss it; greeting everyone at least civilly; showing respect in the way people are addressed.
2. Give credit where credit is due, and let it be known that this has been done.
3. Give as much notice as possible of the looming danger of extra hours having to be worked.
4. Show sufficient interest in colleagues to note when one of them seems ill, worried, under stress, confused or in any other way impaired.
5. Communicate good news or appreciation from on high to everyone concerned, rather than hogging it to yourself.
6. Suppress rumours or gossip – all of which will eventually have a negative effect on morale and leave a nasty taste in the mouth, however piquant they may seem at the time.
7. Consult people before decisions are made – especially those that will directly concern them.
8. Listen to what people have to say, rather than giving the impression that there really isn't time.
9. Encourage people to work together where appropriate. Cooperative working is the foundation stone of good team dynamics.
10. Generally behave as though the team exists.

> TO HANDLE YOURSELF, USE YOUR HEAD;
> TO HANDLE OTHERS, USE YOUR HEART.
> Eleanor Roosevelt

Once the team is assembled it has to be constantly nourished, the more so since its composition may regularly change. Good managers keep a mental or written checklist of what they should do to provide this nourishment. Failure to give people a chance to talk about their work will almost invariably lead to their feeling a lack of appreciation, however lofty their position in the hierarchy of the company.

Saying Thank You

Those who deserve praise and don't get it have a habit of disappearing and joining rival companies, and by then it's too late to acknowledge their value. Anyone who performs his or her task cooperatively, efficiently, thoughtfully and loyally deserves more than just their regular salary and a few brief words of thanks at the annual Christmas get-together.

Whatever your own position in the office, you should be ready to thank anyone who takes a phone call on your behalf or who stays behind to deal with an extra workload. Be grateful to colleagues who show concern when they can see that something is wrong. Always acknowledge people who remember something that you've forgotten.

And don't forget to thank people who lend you things, who clear up your rubbish, and who even offer to make you the occasional cup of tea!

Encouraging Innovation

Management should be receptive to, and appreciative of, new ideas from junior members of staff, whether these ideas are good or bad, old or new, commercial or social. Anyone who thinks they have a way of making office life better or of ensuring a rosy financial future for the company should be listened to with respect.

Presenting Ideas

If you're presenting a new idea make sure that the idea is coherent, and check that it is relevant, new and constructive. Think about how to present it – a little rehearsal can help.

Once you have selected the correct person to present it to, make an appointment to see this person and give some brief idea of what will be on the agenda when this meeting takes place.

Listen to what response is made. If the new idea seems to pass the first hurdle, ask what happens next.

Always make sure credit is given to any colleagues who have been party to the new idea.

Receiving Ideas

Show that you welcome the opportunity to listen to new ideas. Always acknowledge that the idea is a good one, if it is. Use gentle dissuasion if it is not workable. Avoid rash or unrealistic promises, but be sure to carry out whatever promises are made to further the progress of the idea (nothing dispirits a workforce more than empty promises, whether they're about pay rises, security of employment, better work conditions or whatever).

If the powers that be love the idea, be honest about its origins. Seek to involve as many people as possible in sharing the good news if the idea is a success. But avoid the temptation to use one person's success as a stick with which to beat the rest of the office staff who haven't come up with any innovative suggestions.

Office Hierarchies

Teamwork should always be the goal if you want to maintain a creative, happy office atmosphere. But there is no getting away from the fact that – no matter how cooperatively your team works – office hierarchies do exist and must be acknowledged.

As well as knowing the status of everyone in the office it's also important to know the correct way to address everybody – especially bosses. It's possible to pick up a great many clues from other people – but it would be unwise to rely on this approach. Everyone else may have been in the office for years and may have had to earn the right to call the boss by his nickname. It's a fairly safe generalisation to say that the higher up a person is within the company, the less likely they are to welcome being called by his or her nickname. It is best to wait for the invitation to do so from the person concerned.

Familiarity vs. Formality

First names are the order of the day in the vast majority of offices in the UK. A more complicated situation may arise in an office where seniors adopt a two-level or situation-specific approach. This is where they are happy to be called by their first names in the privacy of their own office but wish still to be addressed formally when in front of other members of staff or clients.

Inevitably, social boundaries are re-drawn when everyone is together in the pub after work on a Friday or celebrating some great company success. What matters is that these changes never go too far. The borderline between familiarity and overfamiliarity is very, very finely drawn, to be crossed at your peril. Tread carefully and use your social antennae.

Gaining Access to Senior Staff

It is bad manners to assume that anyone has time to deal with your problems or queries, complaints or requests at any hour of the day; it's professionally unsound to assume that your boss is always available. It is, therefore, a bad idea to buttonhole your boss as he/she dashes past, demanding that they give you their full attention.

If you are dealing with a matter of urgency, then it's permissible to say that you need to see them and to ask politely how quickly that could be arranged.

In normal circumstances, you will need to go through the proper channels and make an appointment to see the boss, either directly or through his/her personal assistant – whatever the office protocols recommend.

Attitudes to Peers and Colleagues

Don't assume that, just because some action doesn't bother you, it won't annoy others – leaving caps off pens, dumping untidy piles of papers on a desk, not putting things back in drawers, etc. Colleagues can easily become upset by this sort of behaviour; of course they're aware that it's not a grave crime, but they feel sensitive to the lack of consideration shown towards them, interpreting it as evidence that you don't value them, which can cause much ill feeling.

Office life can throw all sorts of incompatible people together in close proximity and it is important that everyone finds ways of rubbing along together and getting the job done. Festering resentments and dislikes need to be curbed, and that means adopting restrained patterns of behaviour:

1. Treat no one as an enemy (this doesn't mean treating everyone as a friend).
2. Adopt an attitude of well-mannered amicability towards everyone.
3. Unless and until you learn to the contrary, assume that everyone is honest, means well, and is doing his or her best.
4. If a colleague asks for help, you should either give it, or take the time to explain why this is not possible.

Welcoming New Staff

The company should have a well-established policy and framework for introducing new staff to the workplace. This applies at all levels. Staff who are happy in their workplace will be keen to take on responsibility for initiating new colleagues into the office culture.

Whoever is starting work should have someone deputed to look after them, to introduce them to their new colleagues, and generally to show them the ropes. This designated employee should note when the newcomer is starting and be ready to greet them and give them some time.

A conducted tour is essential – no one should have to work out basic information, such as the location of the loos, meeting room, kitchen, emergency exits, for themselves. The newcomer should be accompanied to his or her desk, and introduced to the people with whom he or she will be working more closely.

Anyone starting in the new workplace needs a lot of information about such matters as phones, computers, office hours, lunch breaks, stationery, health and safety, storage, and a great deal more.

Phones

In the interest of efficiency, it helps if the newcomer knows how the phone system works, how to make internal and external calls, how to transfer calls, access voicemail and so on.

If the company prefers a certain formula for answering phones, explain it to the newcomer at the outset.

Computers

Newcomers should be adequately briefed on office computer systems: shared servers, video meeting systems, available software, back-up protocols and so on. Most importantly, they should be introduced to, or at the very least, given the number of, technical support.

The Cultural Low-Down

This is a good time to hint about the office culture to the newcomer. If prolonged lunchtime exits are frowned upon, or absolute punctuality is expected, it is helpful to convey this to them.

No employer should assume a newcomer knows what the office practice is with regard to working hours. More and more, people are expected to work the hours that it takes to do their job.

Monitoring Newcomers

Welcoming newcomers goes much further than just conducting the office tour and introducing colleagues.

It's important to keep an eye on newcomers and make sure that they settle in. Ask occasionally how things are. This can be a helpful way for a newcomer to voice whatever they're unsure or worried about.

Make sure that you and your colleagues are including newcomers in general invitations – to lunch, drinks and so on. If you are refused, don't take umbrage; the first few weeks at an office can be an exhausting time and it will take some people a while to adjust and feel socially comfortable.

It may well be a good idea to schedule time for a review of how things are going a few weeks after starting.

Offering Help

It should be made clear to all newcomers at the outset where they should go for help and advice. If a newcomer seeks help, it should be given willingly, ungrudgingly and unpatronisingly. If a newcomer is clearly floundering but hasn't sought help, it is both polite and appropriate to offer assistance.

If a newcomer is making clear mistakes, the right reaction is to intervene and explain, rather than to take the matter out of their hands, or to sit back, fold the arms and let a smile of superiority slide over the face.

THE ADVICE THAT IS WANTED IS COMMONLY NOT WELCOME AND THAT WHICH IS NOT WANTED, EVIDENTLY AN EFFRONTERY.

SAMUEL JOHNSON

How to Behave as a Newcomer

Working in a new office means there is a lot to be learned. Everyone takes time to adjust. There are new names to be put to new faces, new routines and new systems to be assimilated, and there is a new ethos to which the newcomer has to adapt.

This is why consideration needs to be shown to any new recruit to a company. At the same time, the new recruit has to make sure that exhaustion and bewilderment aren't likely to be interpreted as distant, uninterested or insensitive behaviour.

Ask for Help when You Need It

Your first few days in an office are not a test to see how you perform under pressure. So if you feel confused by office procedures, puzzled by the photocopiers, and completely outwitted by the computer system, don't just sit tight, trying to tough it out.

Single out a kind, helpful person – very possibly the colleague who was given the task of welcoming you – and indicate that you need some help. It's best to do this diplomatically, perhaps saying 'When you've got a moment, I wonder if you could help? I'm a bit stuck...', rather than marching up to their desk and saying 'I don't know how to unjam the photocopier...'

What matters is not how many mistakes a newcomer makes, but how quickly he or she learns from them.

When in Rome…

If the general tone of the office is quiet and reserved, then boisterously friendly overtures on the part of the newcomer may be out of place and unwelcome. Respect other people's private space and property and be careful about borrowing their possessions. If the general impression is that staff in the office keep themselves very much to themselves, then this has to be respected, even if it doesn't seem the right way to work.

Similarly, if the office buzzes with chatter and banter, then an unyieldingly frigid response to every overture of friendship isn't appropriate. Most workplaces have a detectable culture, covering such diverse questions as informal socialising after-hours and willingly stepping in to alleviate a colleague's workload. The newcomer ignores this at his or her peril.

The likelihood is, of course, that the personnel of any office constitute a mixed bunch. Some will keep themselves very much to themselves, others will be insatiably nosy, many will take up a position somewhere between these two extremes.

There will be those who wish to initiate the new recruit into the office gossip, and they should be treated with extreme caution. Over-eagerness to find out about the gossip and even join in might mean that you fall foul of important people; gossip is particularly dangerous for the uninitiated who do not yet know the ins and outs of office culture. Remain polite but make your excuses and leave, perhaps indicating that you have other things to do.

Pushing New Ideas

A newcomer may be bursting to communicate how much better he or she handled matters at a previous workplace. There are few things worse than the daily frustration of knowing that it's possible to work faster and more efficiently but not being allowed to do so.

Tact is needed here. Again it's a matter of going to the right person (whoever has the authority to implement such changes) and starting up a conversation. It's also not a bad idea to have a memo prepared on the subject, in case the person to whom the brilliant new idea is entrusted tries to steal it.

CHAPTER 05

PUNCTUALITY

This is perhaps the single issue that causes the most complaints, resentment and animosity within offices. It has to be accepted that in the world of business, as in everyday life, punctuality matters enormously. To be late for an interview, a meeting, a conference, a business lunch or just work, without having a good reason that has been communicated to the relevant parties, is a grave fault and universally considered to be bad manners. Being late is not a sign of importance or great industry. It is a sign of poor organisation, or thoughtlessness, or rudeness.

Late for Work

All instances of unpunctuality call for an apology, but different circumstances call for different action to accompany that apology. Run of the mill lateness for work should be acknowledged and accompanied by apologies to colleagues as well as an immediate superior. They may have had to cover for you and have had extra work thrust upon them. They may have had to work in an atmosphere soured by your failing to turn up on time. The apology should be accompanied by a very brief explanation of why you were late – transport, childcare, domestic emergency etc. You should also demonstrate concern for any impact your lateness may have had on your colleagues.

Late for Appointments

If you are late for an appointment then the priority above all others is to use your mobile phone to get a message through to the person you are meeting (or the lead person, if you are meeting a group) to let them know that you are going to be late. If possible you should speak to the person to whom this most matters and you should try and give a reasonable estimate of just how late you are going to be. It is polite to try and speak to the person concerned; if they are not picking up, then leave a text message, which should be clearly written and fully explanatory. If you are going to be very late, then you have to consider whether or not to offer cancelling or postponing the appointment.

Knowing that you are not going to be at the office in time to greet a visitor is more complicated. You still have to alert the visitor as quickly as possible, but you also must brief someone to act on your behalf. Once you find someone at the office to help you out (for example by greeting the visitor and offering tea or other refreshments), then you should contact your visitor and apologise and explain who will be greeting them. You should also give an accurate forecast of when you will arrive. Depending on how late you are running, you should also offer them the opportunity to postpone or cancel the appointment if they so wish.

It is not good manners to ask someone to lie on your behalf, or pass on an inadequate excuse, or have to invent some wild and unlikely story.

Letting People Know

Lateness usually arrives unexpectedly, but there can be days when you know in advance that you are going to be late. You may have to visit a child's school, take the car to the garage or attend a dental appointment, for example. Because you know in advance, you are not so much telling people that you are going to be late as asking if it is acceptable. It's only polite to ask permission of a manager, and check first with colleagues to ensure that your lateness will not create difficulties for them. Try and give as much notice as possible; telling everyone as you leave the office that you're going to be late the following morning may lead to bad feelings.

If a change in your personal circumstances, for example a new baby or house move, means that you need to make radical adjustments to your working hours, you should consult with your employers at the earliest possible opportunity, giving details of what changes are requested, why, and for how long. Unless it's commercially impossible for the employers to agree, they should do all they can to accommodate these requests.

Smoothing the Way

Whenever difficulties arise, everyone should do their utmost to minimise difficulties, avoid embarrassment, pre-empt problems, forestall anger. This is the cornerstone of good business etiquette.

BETTER THREE HOURS TOO SOON THAN A MINUTE TOO LATE.

Oscar Wilde

Dealing with Latecomers

The persistent latecomer in an office can be a source of much bitterness, but a soft answer may turn away sloth as well as wrath:

1. Discover why the offender is persistently late – this may need both patience and perseverance.

2. If the offender has a good reason, treat the matter with concern – the aim is first and foremost to solve the problem, not punish the offender.

3. If the offender hasn't a good reason, firmly but politely outline why the lateness is unacceptable.

4. If the offender shows no signs of remorse, or, even worse, of changing his or her ways, then disciplinary action is the only way forward.

5. If the first step is a warning, make sure it is clear and understood.

The role of colleagues in this sorry saga is a little different. Having no powers of discipline and control, all colleagues can do is exhort latecomers to mend their ways, and explain how everyone in the office is adversely affected. This, again, should be done politely. Whether the occasion calls for a quiet word with a diplomatic colleague, or whether it's a case of everyone pitching in with their own contribution, will depend on the nature and attitude of the offender and all concerned. Whichever approach is favoured, it should be seen as an attempt to solve a problem.

Excuses and How to Handle Them

One of the few things that all of us learn at a young age is that there is a right way and a wrong way to make an excuse or to tender an apology. To be successful the excuse must have some basis in truth (the more, the better). It should be used with discretion, ie not too often, and should sound plausible. It should never be accompanied by misplaced attempts at humour.

Everybody has to make an excuse at some time or another, not least when they are unpunctual, and the best thing they can do is make the excuse with as good grace as possible.

All discussions about transgressions such as unpunctuality should take place in private. It is possible that the offender has a perfectly valid reason for their misdemeanour, but does not want their colleagues to hear what it is. If any criticisms or rebukes are to be delivered they should be for the recipient's ears alone.

A reasonable excuse should be accepted, without rancour or resentment, and it is fair enough to point out any complications that have arisen for the company as a result of the aberrant behaviour. This may be necessary because it has had an effect on other staff that needs explanation and appreciation.

If the excuse is made repeatedly then there may well come a time when, although the excuse is accepted, a dialogue has to be opened up as to how much longer these difficulties will continue. Discussions may centre around the possibility of establishing alternative hours, of passing responsibility for some work to another person, of granting paid or unpaid leave for a fixed period or seeing if there are any other ways in which the problem can be solved or ameliorated.

If the excuse is not a reasonable one then it has to be rejected. The manner of this rejection will probably depend on just how unreasonable the excuse is and the attitude and track record of the offender. It should be remembered, however, that some people make unreasonable or lame excuses simply because they are afraid to reveal the real reason why they are late or have been absent. This can be especially true when private or family life is going awry. If someone who is in all other ways a valued member of the company starts to behave with unaccustomed irresponsibility and offers unlikely excuses, the company needs to reject only the excuses, not the person making them. No company ever gains prestige through rudeness or insensitivity towards clients, customers or employees.

> I NEVER COULD HAVE DONE WHAT I HAVE DONE WITHOUT THE HABITS OF PUNCTUALITY, ORDER, AND DILIGENCE, WITHOUT THE DETERMINATION TO CONCENTRATE MYSELF ON ONE SUBJECT AT A TIME.
> CHARLES DICKENS

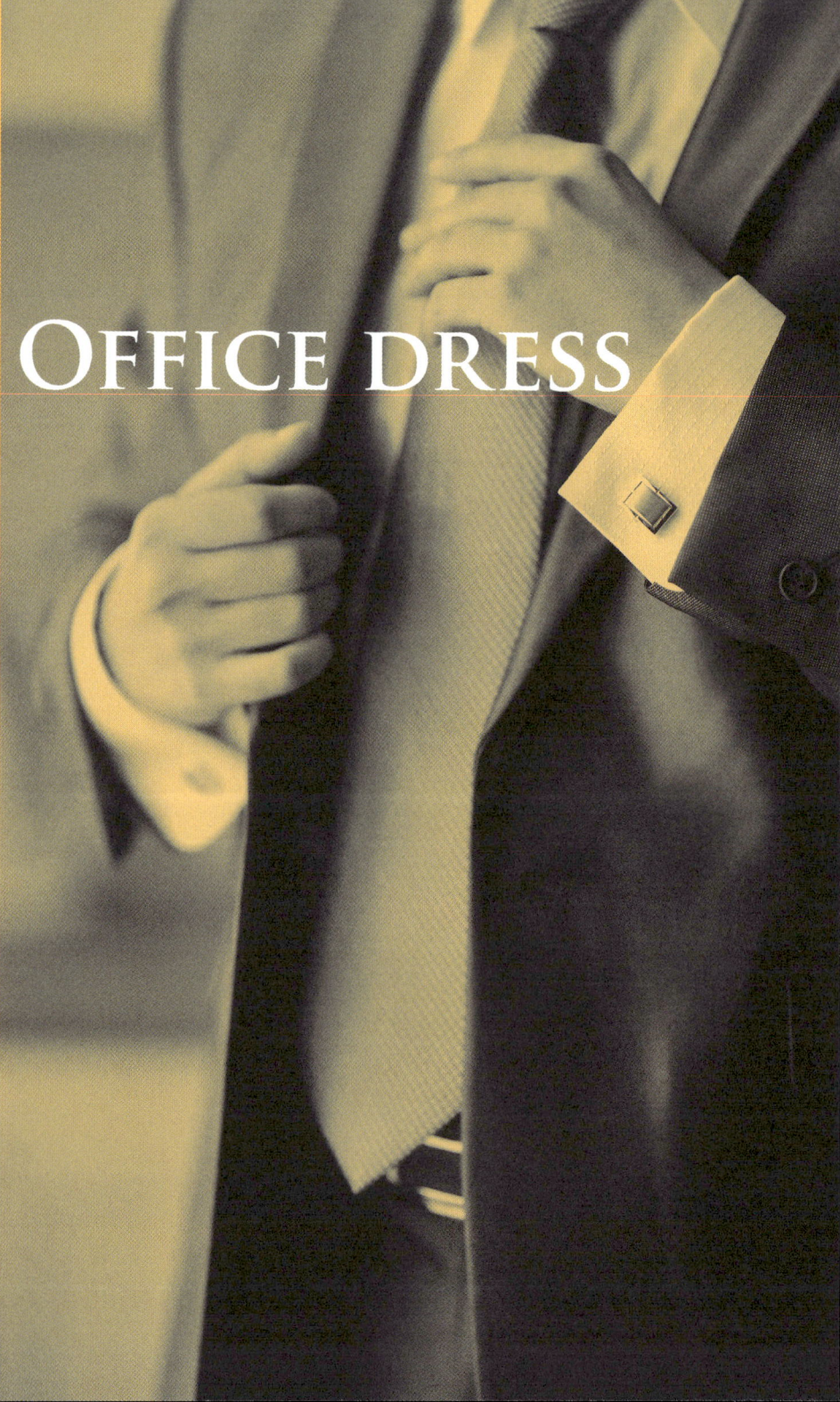

OFFICE DRESS

CHAPTER 06

OFFICE DRESS | 63

This is a vexed question for many employees, and it involves being sensitive to the office environment and using your powers of observation.

The days when armies of be-suited and bowler-hatted workers swarmed out of London's large commuter stations in a uniformed throng are now over. British office dress now covers the entire gamut, from extremely casual to smart and formal.

The trick is to pick up on clues about the prevailing office dress culture, and to conform to that perceived culture. Unless you work in fashion or the arts, offices really aren't places where you should make a song and dance about asserting your flamboyance and individuality; save that for weekends.

Certain offices are more likely to adhere to more formal dress codes: for example, traditional City institutions such as banks, insurance offices, or stockbrokers.

At the other end of the spectrum, the creative industries (newspapers, magazines, tv production companies, design agencies) are likely to be extremely casual, with no discernible difference between office dress and weekend wear.

DRESS SHABBILY AND THEY REMEMBER THE DRESS; DRESS IMPECCABLY AND THEY NOTICE THE WOMAN.

Coco Chanel

Formal Office Wear

These are broad guidelines for workspaces that are perceived to be more formal and traditional. It goes without saying that accessories, such as shoes and ties, can make or break a formal outfit, and should not be overlooked.

Men

VERY FORMAL
- Dark suit
- Shirt and tie
- Dark shoes, laced-up

SLIGHTLY LESS FORMAL
- Jacket
- Shirt, without tie
- Chino-style trousers (not jeans)
- brogues, loafers, laced-up shoes

Women

VERY FORMAL
- Dark suit (trousers)
- Dark suit (skirt)
- Tailored dress with matching jacket
- Dark court shoes with a mid-sized heel

SLIGHTLY LESS FORMAL
- Skirt
- Tailored trousers
- Blouse or buttoned shirt (not t-shirt)
- Dress (though not too tent-like or voluminous)
- Jacket
- Leather shoes (flat, kitten-heeled or stilettos) or smart boots

The above-listed clothes all play safe and will not cause offence. They are a useful default position, and it would be a good idea to wear them for interviews. You may sense at the interview that you are overly-formally dressed, but nobody will condemn you for this, because it looks as if you are taking the interview seriously and making an effort, and there is a general expectation that job candidates will do so. You can downplay the formality if you actually get the job.

Clothes that are Best Avoided

While there are certainly workplaces where it's fine to wear jeans and t-shirts, the following items are best avoided:

- Shorts
- track-suit bottoms
- jogging tops
- trainers
- flip-flops

Grooming

While in many offices it is certainly not expected for you to look as if you have just emerged from a barber's or beauty salon, looking reasonably well-groomed and well-laundered is a basic requirement across the board.

This means washing and brushing your hair, ensuring that your nails are clean and trimmed, and checking clothes to make sure that there are no food stains or unsightly creases.

Women who wear tights might do well to keep a spare pair in their desk drawer, as ladders look unduly scruffy.

If you jog, speed-walk or cycle to work, allow yourself enough time to change out of lycra, trainers, tracksuits etc., brush your hair and acquire a smooth, unflurried persona.

Bear in mind that dressing for work is not just about complying with office conventions. If you look reasonably well turned out and present a well-maintained façade to the world, it will enhance your image in the office, and you will radiate confidence.

Looking unkempt and untidy may sow the seeds of doubt in the minds of your colleagues and bosses, who may well associate your dishevelled appearance with an untidy and chaotic mind.

DRESSING WELL IS A FORM OF GOOD MANNERS.

TOM FORD

CHAPTER 07

OFFICE RELATIONSHIPS

Offices are primarily places of work, but they are also social hothouses, where a range of people, often ill-assorted, are forced to spend many hours together. In fact, many workaholics freely admit that they spend more hours per day with their colleagues than with their family.

Clearly, in these highly charged circumstances, promoting social harmony is paramount. Inevitably, people will single each other out as close friends, and in some circumstances, lovers. It is important that these close relationships do not disrupt the wider office community.

Not everyone will get on, and unfortunately incidences of bullying, gossip and scandal-mongering occur in offices from time to time.

It is the job of office managers to observe these social dynamics, encourage a friendly and supportive atmosphere, and intervene promptly and decisively when relationships sour.

Office Friendships

No one should ever feel less welcome, less valued, less trusted or less promising a member of a team simply because they do not share a friendship.

If you introduce a friend to the office, help him or her get a job alongside you, there is always the grave risk that you will give that friend preferential treatment. This is not simply a case of trying to advance your friend's career at the expense of other colleagues. It's a matter of day-to-day behaviour. The same problems can arise when firm friendships are made within the office context. If two colleagues bond closely, they may appear to present an exclusive and united front, which excludes and alienates other members of the team.

Here are some examples of what constitutes discourteous behaviour in this situation:

1. Sharing private jokes with a friend.
2. Spending much break time (and work time) audibly recalling what you and your friend have been doing at the weekend or the night before.
3. Indicating that there exists a private world, with 'special' names for members of the office staff and a 'special' way of looking at what happens in the office.
4. Giving the friend favoured treatment, eg being prepared to stay late to help a friend when you have steadfastly refused to help out others in the past.
5. Forgiving your friend his or her trespasses (lateness, signing off early, incompetence) when you are unforgiving towards everyone else.
6. Choosing the best or easiest bits of work for a friend.
7. Expecting everyone else to give the friend preferential treatment.
8. Flaunting the friendship in front of everyone else.

As well as the problems that might crop up while you are working with a friend, there is always the problem of what happens if the friendship starts to go sour. This is why it's so important not to let the friendship interfere with work or with good office practice.

ALL HUMAN BEINGS HAVE THREE LIVES: PUBLIC, PRIVATE, AND SECRET.

Gabriel García Márquez

Office Romance

Falling in love or lust can cause all sorts of problems in an office – for the rest of the staff if not for the lovers. People in love tend to do silly things. They forget that there are other people in the world, other important events, other pressing needs. They believe, albeit subconsciously, that they can attend to their duties with a mind that is at best limping along on 25 per cent of normal concentration. And above all they are oblivious of almost everything around them and unaware that their behaviour is being closely observed and monitored by critical colleagues.

Notes for Office Lotharios

1. Lovers shouldn't expect everyone else to share in their joy.
2. Work has to come before passion in paid office time.
3. There is always a limit to people's patience, and the limit is usually nearer than lovers imagine.
4. Lovers often go hand in hand. Love and promotion seldom do.
5. If the affair comes to an end it may be impossible to go on working together. If the affair doesn't come to an end it may also be impossible to go on working together.

There are no rules about the degree of intimacy permissible in an office. The onus is on the lovers to make themselves aware of the feelings of others. It may be acceptable to enter the office holding hands, it may not, so better not to risk it. Broadly speaking, the more the relationship is kept under control, the happier the rest of the office will be.

To handle yourself, use your head; to handle others, use your heart.
Eleanor Roosevelt

Even more complications arise when the passion crosses strata within the office hierarchy – for example when a boss falls for a junior. The best thing for the parties involved to do is keep quiet about the whole thing. A private secret is better than public resentment. Once such an affair becomes notorious, both parties will be subject to intense scrutiny, and any failure to carry out their jobs will be roundly condemned. Should either or both of the parties already be married, then the condemnation will be bitter.

Illicit affairs in the office – when married colleagues form a relationship – pose particular problems. They may well put colleagues who know the spouses of the individuals concerned in a particularly invidious position, and therefore the couple involved should do their utmost not to embarrass or compromise their co-workers.

How to Deal with Office Lovers

If the couple are behaving with some sense of decorum and propriety, it doesn't hurt to be tolerant. If they aren't, then you have to bring this to their attention in a firm but gentle way.

This needs to be done privately and tactfully. It also needs to be done to the offending pair, not just to one party. Who delivers the rebuke is open to debate. If there is someone with responsibility for office management then clearly it may be regarded as their job. But there is sometimes a case to be made for an alternative and more informal approach – for example, a friend of the couple may have a private word.

People in an office shouldn't have to spend any part of their working day keeping their heads down to avoid seeing something that would embarrass them. Nor should they have to make snap moral judgements about whether it is appropriate to approve or disapprove of what is essentially private behaviour.

THE PERFECT LOVE AFFAIR IS ONE WHICH IS CONDUCTED ENTIRELY BY POST.

GEORGE BERNARD SHAW

Keep it Private

If you become romantically involved with a colleague at the office, the simplest way to avoid a scandal is to leave that romance outside the office; the further away the better. Here are a few precautionary reminders to office sweethearts:

1. Don't think public transport is safe – others from the office may use the same route occasionally if not regularly.

2. Office lovers should not give or send cards or flowers to each other on birthdays, unless intending to do the same for everyone else in the office.

3. When alone in a room, office lovers should remember that it is never possible to spring apart in time when someone else comes in.

4. Office radar is highly effective; you may think you're being discreet but your colleagues will undoubtedly be on to you.

5. One of the commonest early indications of romance is a deterioration in work standards clear to all.

6. Be very guarded about making phone calls to your lover when you're at your desk; audibly whispering sweet nothings will alienate your colleagues.

7. All the world loves a lover except where time and money are involved.

Bullying in the Office

Just as special relationships within the office can cause problems, victimising and hounding one particular member of staff, or turning one individual into the office scapegoat, can severely impact the cohesion and harmony of the workplace.

Workplace bullying can cover a range of behaviour: verbal abuse, intrusive questions, offensive or sexual remarks, jokes or innuendo-laden remarks made at an individual's expense. It can happen between colleagues, or a boss can bully a junior.

Some bullying is a group phenomenon: a group of individuals bond together to isolate or freeze out a colleague.

It is generally considered that behaviour is bullying if it is humiliating, offensive, intimidating, hostile or degrading. It can often be a fine line between a tough boss and an abusive one, but this line has to be drawn. Bullies, when called out, will often adopt the 'can't you take a joke or a bit of banter?' defence, but this is open to challenge.

If you are suffering from bullying and there are witnesses, it can be very useful to elicit their opinion. If the bullying takes place in a private context, explain what has happened and seek the advice of an objective friend. Make a record of what has happened, including examples of offensive remarks. The main priority is to report the problem to a manager, or to Human Resources, and to give them clear instances – and evidence, if it exists – of the behaviour.

Cyberbullying

Unfortunately, in our online world, bullies have a whole range of new weapons in their armoury. They can take their bullying online, or onto the office intranet, or social networking sites, sharing photos for the purpose of ridicule, spreading scandal and scurrilous rumours, or creating groups that exclude the victim. They can use a shield of anonymity to undermine their targets or even create bogus profiles, which they can use to persecute them.

How to Deal with Bullying

Employers are responsible for the wellbeing of their employees. As with all office behaviour, managers need to be vigilant about bullying. They should never condone the behaviour in the belief that 'robust' business relationships get results.

In the first instance, you should, of course, talk to the bully, making it clear that their behaviour has been observed and is considered unacceptable. If you have evidence of a case of bullying in the office, it needs to be nipped in the bud, otherwise the situation will escalate and other staff will feel intimidated and demotivated. You need to make it clear to all your staff that you are committed to promoting dignity and respect at work.

Of course, if the bullying persists after you have spoken to the culprit, you may have to escalate procedures against him or her, from written warnings, to suspension and ultimately dismissal.

Harassment

This is bullying behaviour that falls clearly under the remit of employment law. It is unwanted conduct affecting the dignity of men and women in the workplace and it may be related to age, gender, maternity or pregnancy, race, disability, religion, sexual orientation, nationality or any personal characteristic. It may be persistent, or an isolated incident. The key factor is that the actions or comments are viewed as demeaning and unacceptable to the recipient, and/or create a hostile environment for the recipient.

Any employee can report a harassment issue they've seen or heard at work, even if it is not directed at them. In the first instance, reports should be made to managers, HR or union representatives. If this is not followed up, a formal complaint may be made using the employer's grievance procedure. The ultimate sanction is to take legal action at an employment tribunal.

> We explain when someone is cruel or acts like a bully, you do not stoop to their level. Our motto is when they go low, you go high.
> Michelle Obama

Scandal, Rumour and Gossip

In any large office, at any given time, there is usually a rumour to be picked up, but you should resist the temptations to join in the company tittle-tattle.

We all have our moments of weakness when we join the gossiping throng, with cries of 'did he really? …', and an occasional lapse is generally forgivable, but there are those who make a regular practice of maligning others or of spreading morale-lowering misinformation about the future of the company. Gaining a reputation as a rumour-monger or gossip is not a wise career move. For a while you may be the centre of attention at every tea break; sooner or later the rumour will reach the wrong ears, and then there will be trouble.

Offices are places where rumours about the future of the company, redundancies, shutdowns, mergers, takeovers, bankruptcies and all the other joys of the business world thrive.

It is difficult or impossible to ignore such rumours. For your own peace of mind, the best thing you can do is to try to trace the rumour back to its source. Who said it? Where did they say it, when did they say it? There is nothing wrong with such detective work. A little tact or diplomacy may have to be used in how it's done.

If the rumour comes from a public source – a news website, newspaper, Twitter or television report – then there is all the more justification in seeking denial or confirmation. It is not a good idea, however, to assume that all we read or hear is true.

GOSSIP IS WHAT NO ONE CLAIMS TO LIKE, BUT EVERYBODY ENJOYS.

Joseph Conrad

Gagging Gossip

If you are in a position of authority, then you are entitled to take all reasonable steps to try to stop gossip proliferating. If you know who is responsible for the rumour-mongering, then you can confront them about what they are doing. If there is an element of truth in the rumour, then this may not be easy, and you may have to embark on a damage-limitation exercise. It may be the best you can do is appeal to whoever is spreading the rumour to stop, on the grounds that it is causing embarrassment or worse to the company. If the rumour is totally false, you may feel free to issue orders and threaten sanctions if the guilty party doesn't comply.

For those of us who aren't in a position of authority, there are other options open. You may wish to display a 'holier than thou' attitude, showing that you are aware of the rumours flying around, but that you are choosing to take no notice of them. But there are occasions when the rumour is potentially harmful to the collective or the individual, and turning a deaf ear isn't the right thing to do. In such cases one procedure is to ask the perpetrator to stop, and, if necessary, retract what they have been saying. If they don't, then you should raise the matter with the relevant authority, making sure that the culprit knows that this is what you are doing. This may sound a little prudish, but misinformation is a deadly weapon, whether it's used deliberately or negligently. People's lives have been ruined by it and companies have gone under as a result of it.

Tolerating Gossip

Any employer would be foolish to aspire to an office where there is absolutely not a whisper of gossip. An office is a random collection of human beings, forced into close proximity. Many workers see more of their colleagues, day to day, than their spouse or children. It is therefore inevitable, and only human, that they will display curiosity about each other.

A certain amount of benign gossip is probably a useful device, which promotes camaraderie and team spirit. It may be gossip to speculate about a colleague's marriage plans, house purchase or relationship break-up, but it is not particularly damaging if the chit-chat is reasonably amiable and non-malicious, and may have the positive effect of enhancing relationships. The line is inevitably crossed when somebody's feelings are hurt by scurrilous rumours, or when team morale is suffering.

Fighting Back

If you are a victim of rumours or gossip you may be tempted to ignore it, worried perhaps that your denial may appear too forceful. In general, however, it's best to step in quickly. Rumour-mongering can be like a drug in many ways – the longer people are allowed to indulge in it, the harder it becomes to give up. And, although there may be the fear that by contradicting the rumour you are actually giving it some kind of validity, your silence would in most cases be interpreted as proof that there was some truth in the rumour.

If you don't know the source of the scandal, or if your attempts to scotch it are ineffective, then you have to take more serious action. You should go to a manager and explain to him or her what is happening – this is based on the assumption that the rumour is in fact true, but it may be the right thing to do even if it isn't.

If the gossip is not stifled, then you may ask your managers to make sure that something is done about it, or you will consider bringing the problem to your association or union, or even consider legal action. In many cases merely telling your manager that you are considering legal action may convince them that they should do something to circumvent this. But remember, you should never threaten any action that you are not prepared to take.

One of the best courses of action if you are the victim of rumour is to consult with a colleague whose opinion and advice you really trust. A friend will have a less emotional perspective on the matter, and may be a better judge of what's really happening. They may know that the wisest thing to do is to let the whole affair blow over, or may offer to intervene on your behalf. Remember – if you work in an atmosphere where rumour and gossip appear to go unchecked, then something needs to be done for everyone's sake.

> Any fool can make a lot of noise. But it takes a strong bull to go his own way and forget the things those bullies say.
>
> Walt Disney

CHAPTER 08

OFFICE
SOCIAL LIFE

When people are thrown together in the intense atmosphere of an office, they form relationships, make friends and sometimes, unfortunately, enemies. Most well-run workplaces seek to mitigate the more unfortunate aspects of office relationships by promoting social interaction. This can range from impromptu after-work drinks to working lunches and office parties. In all instances, socialising is a chance to see colleagues outside the diurnal, workaday context, and to relate to them as human beings, with families, homes and outside interests. At best, socialising will help teams to bond and ensure that offices are happier places.

After Hours Socialising

Colleagues at most offices will, from time to time, get together for drinks or grab a quick lunch. They may do so because they have been under pressure, because they're celebrating a success, or simply because it is Friday.

In many instances, these gatherings will be impromptu – a spur of the moment idea. But in many offices this kind of socialising is more planned, mainly because it is seen as a useful way of consolidating team spirit and helping colleagues to bond with each other.

This is undoubtedly a useful device for the manager, but they will need to be sensitive, when planning these regular events, to the possibility that a very regular commitment may seem oppressive to some team-members, especially if they have a busy home life (small children for example). You do not want to put people in a position where they feel that refusing to socialise will jeopardise their work reputation. If this is a danger, why not consider a regular lunch (it could even be sandwiches in the office), which will help with team-building without making demands on employees' free time.

If you are an employee in a convivial office, where drinks are frequently mooted and after-hours socialising is the norm, do your best to participate, at least some of the time. You may not always be able, or willing, to join in, but a modicum of sociability will mean that you are perceived as a team-player, not a lone wolf.

Work is the curse of the drinking classes.
Oscar Wilde

Socialising at Office Parties

Business entertaining is a complex subject, and it may help to start by establishing some general principles:

1 Whether it's a party, a lunch, a trip to the theatre, a farewell gathering or whatever, there has to be a reason for the function and hopefully a purpose to it.

2 No one should ever be forced to attend a celebration. Refuseniks should not be nagged or pressurised.

3 Since, therefore, you are attending of our own volition, you should at least appear to be having a good time.

4 Few good parties are created spontaneously – preparation and planing helps.

5 Whatever your own personal preferences in terms of what constitutes a great party, if you have been given the task of organising a party, you have to consider what others might like.

6 If outsiders are invited to a party, someone should be given the task of looking after them.

The Office 'Party'

This might not inevitably be a traditional party, and smaller-scale alternatives are certainly an option. A trip to the theatre, an excursion on a river boat, or a dinner in a restaurant are all feasible alternatives – a restaurant dinner, for example, can be a godsend to the less extrovert members of staff. For those who still prefer the traditional office party there are a number of dos and don'ts:

- Make an effort to decorate the room in which the party is taking place so that it looks welcoming and festive, not functional.

- Try to help those who are shy to have a good time.

- Similarly, if you are shy at least try to join in the fun.

- Don't leave all the preparations to the one or two noble volunteers who did it last year and the year before that. And don't leave all the clearing up to them either.

- It helps if some indication is given (on invitations etc) as to what the purpose of the party is – to get together in an informal and friendly fashion, to mark the festive season, to enable members of the departments to meet or whatever. If the party has an expressed purpose, then there is less chance of it getting wildly out of hand.

- Don't force people to drink. There is nothing criminal or sinister about those who believe they can have a good time on sparkling mineral water.

The office party is not the time to buttonhole the boss or head of department to tell them what you think of them, or fellow workers, to demand a raise, to confront them with the Dickensian conditions in which you toil. Neither is it the time to grab the boss by the lapels and reveal a wonderful new invention/formula/plan. It's certainly isn't the time to ingratiate yourself with your boss, pleading for advancement, listing your impressive qualities and qualifications and badmouthing your colleagues.

Instead, try and impress your boss and your colleagues with your social skills. Make every effort to circulate, do not get bogged down in a clique, or spend the evening with your team. Introduce yourself to people from other departments, assist fellow-guests with drinks and food, keep an eye open for social wallflowers.

Mixing Work and Play

Office parties are inevitably occasions when the barrier between work and social life breaks down and, undoubtedly aided by alcohol, there can be interesting consequences. Reticence evaporates, tongues loosen, confidences and gossip are exchanged, revelations are made. Frequently, and most embarrassingly of all, sexual inhibitions begin to dissipate, and the evening ends in a flurry of passes and unexpected liaisons.

The morning after an office social debacle can be an excruciating affair. The dimly-remembered indiscretions of the night before are the water-cooler and coffee-machine gossip-fodder of the morning after. Walking into an office after an unfortunate social performance takes reserves of insouciance and chutzpah that many of us simply don't possess.

So, remember the limitations of office life. Save your wildest, most uninhibited behaviour for your friends, and ration your intake of the demon drink at the work social. You may come across as demure and self-contained, but at least you'll be able to hold your head up the following morning.

If indiscretions have occurred, what are you going to do about it? The average office party sin (straightforward drunkenness) may be best left without apology; other people may also have been intoxicated and it doesn't help to remind people of what you did – it may easily be forgotten in the mists of alcoholic amnesia. But if you badly overstepped the mark, then it's time to take a deep breath and humble yourself. Make sure of your facts (by making discreet enquiries of a friend) before embarking on the process of apologising. You should know for certain what you did wrong, and to whom you should apologise.

I HAVE BEEN BROUGHT UP AND TRAINED TO HAVE THE UTMOST CONTEMPT FOR PEOPLE WHO GET DRUNK.

WINSTON CHURCHILL

Working Lunches

Working lunches with colleagues may be celebrations of a job well done or business success, or they may be an opportunity to take work out of the office context, and hash out a problem or spark creative ideas assisted by food, drink and conviviality.

Whatever the reason for the lunch, much the same rules prevail. It is essential that the host is at the venue before the appointed hour. Guests should not have to wait at a restaurant that is probably unknown to them, wondering if they have got the location and time right.

See Business Entertaining see pp 213–17

Ordering Food and Drink

It helps if the host makes some suggestions as to what might be ordered, based on his or her experiences at the restaurant. This is also a good opportunity for the host to give some hints to the guests about how many courses to order and the general parameters of what to choose. If the host says 'I think I'll just go straight to the main course', this is definitely a signal not to order a starter. If he or she opts for a simple pasta dish, now is not the time to toy with an expensive fillet steak.

The same guidance should be followed when ordering drink. If the host says 'shall we have a bottle of wine?' you know that drinking is permissible. If he or she goes straight for mineral water, think twice before ordering wine for yourself.

When you make your food order, bear in mind that you will be observed by your colleagues and you need to maintain a flawless work persona. Don't order food that is messy or difficult to eat; trying to discuss the latest sales figures while strings of tomato-sauce-covered spaghetti dangle from your mouth is not a good look. Tricky shellfish and unfilleted fish may also demand reserves of concentration that you really cannot spare when you're trying to impress your boss.

It is the guests' duty to be appreciative of the food and drink with which they are served. It is the host's duty to make sure that everyone is well looked after. However earnest the conversation may be, however tight the negotiation, however detailed the plans being laid, the host should always take an occasional quick glance round the table to see if anyone appears ill at ease, thirsty, or unhappy with the food in front of them.

When to Leave

At the end of the meal there is sometimes a problem as to when people should depart. Ending the meal with coffee is often a good idea, as that provides a kind of finale. It is perfectly in order for any guest to thank the host for the meal at any time once coffee is served and then depart. If it is clear that one or more guests are reluctant to move, then it is quite in order for the host to explain that he or she has to leave as they have another appointment back at the office. This should be taken by the guests as a signal that the meal is over and that the time has come for all to depart.

> The problem with the world is that everyone is a few drinks behind.
> Humphrey Bogart

Leaving Parties

When a colleague retires, or moves on to new pastures, it is customary to mark the occasion by throwing a small party or at least assembling in the appropriate office to raise a glass and wish him or her well. It is up to the leaver's colleagues to decide how elaborate the farewells should be. This will depend on the amount of time he or she has worked for the company; someone who has been there for decades is entitled to an extravagant celebration, perhaps even a special party.

A member of staff has to be designated to take on the responsibility of organising the event, however humble or elaborate it may be, and of planning a suitable gathering.

Whatever format is deemed suitable, a little pre-thought is necessary. The 'goodbye' should suit the person departing. A shy person will not want fanfares, elaborate toasts and to be called upon to make a speech. Even an extrovert may not welcome a surprise party. Sensitive people may dread being asked to withstand an emotionally charged farewell. It helps to keep a few basic points in mind:

1. Where is the most appropriate venue? The office? Or a nearby bar? Or a restaurant?
2. When is the best time to hold the party? The day the person leaves? A day or two before?
3. Who should be invited? Everyone connected with the departee? Management?
4. How elaborate is the occasion to be? Will there be formal speeches or should it be more informal, with a joking speech about the leaver's eccentricities?
5. If there are going to be formal speeches, who should be asked to make them?
6. Is there to be a collection for a leaving present? Who is going to make the collection? Who is going to be asked to contribute?
7. Once the collection has been made, who will have the task of choosing a suitable gift and who is going to present it?
8. Who is going to clear up when it's all over?

Leaving Presents

Collecting money for a leaving present is a complex business. Contributions should be discreet and anonymous, so a tin or box is the ideal receptacle, ensuring that people can give coins as well as notes (more difficult in an over-stuffed and sagging envelope). You don't want to create an awkward situation where individual contributions are closely scrutinised – extravagant (or stingy) donors will set the tone, making other contributors feel they ought to follow suit. It is much better to privately assess what your able, and willing, to give.

There may well be those who don't wish to contribute – either out of personal animosity towards the person leaving, or because they can't afford to, or they're tight-fisted, or because they've only just joined the company and they've never met the person for whom the collection is being made. In each case there is a chance of causing embarrassment, so it is sometimes better if the word goes around that so-and-so is organising a collection and that they are, therefore, the people to see. This allows those who don't wish to contribute, for whatever reason, the chance to duck out surreptitiously.

Private vs Public

CHAPTER 09

Privacy is a two-way concept. There are the times and places when we must respect the privacy of others within the office, and there are the times and places when we must respect the office and not inflict the details of our private lives on our colleagues.

We should always be alert to occasions when our workmates are to be left alone; if one of our colleagues has indicated that they need some peace and quiet to finish the monthly report, then that wish should be respected. If the occupant of an office usually leaves the door open (a sign that he or she is happy to receive visitors and be interrupted) then we should not barge in when it is closed.

However, office life is no longer a simple matter of closed doors and discreet silences. Online working, and the vast range of digital media platforms now available, means that everyone has myriad ways of connecting, and inevitably a substantial portion of online communication is unrelated to work and challenges our understanding of what is private.

The Phone Dilemma

In the days before mobile phones, the office phone system was probably abused – it was understood that employees were allowed to use the office phone line for private calls, within reason, and certainly there would be no criticism if the phone was used in an emergency. However, sitting at your desk, having a lengthy private chat on the office phone was not considered good business etiquette. It was also an open invitation for colleagues (willingly or unwillingly) to eavesdrop on your private phone calls.

It is much easier today, when we all have mobile phones, to resist the temptation to use the office phones for private conversations. But just because you're using your own phone, and paying for your own calls, don't make the mistake of thinking that it's acceptable to use it whenever the urge takes you. You are employed in an office to work, and employers will take a dim view of loquacious phone-users.

Arguing that you don't care about the right to privacy because you have nothing to hide is no different than saying you don't care about free speech because you have nothing to say.

Edward Snowden

Mobile Phones

We need to ensure that we are using these indispensable items sensibly and discreetly at work.

Follow these simple guidelines:

1. Keep your phone out of sight (preferably in a bag or drawer). If it's on your desk your eye will constantly be drawn to it, and you will find it hard to resist picking it up, looking at it, and fiddling with it.

2. If you receive calls on your mobile that have to be answered, do so away from your desk if possible. You can usually take a call in reception, in a corridor, on the stairs. But keep an eye on the clock and don't get carried away.

3. Put your phone on silent; your colleagues will be irritated by an array of intrusive ringtones, beeps and alerts.

4. Try and rein in your texting habit. If you're constantly hunched over your phone, texting, people will assume that it is not work-related.

5. Try and control your tendency to check the apps on your phone, social media, Facebook etc with alarming frequency. Ration the number of times per day you do so. No employer is going to tolerate an employee who is demonstrably more interested in their social life than their work.

6. Don't carry your phone around when you move about the office, and don't take it into meetings. Never put it on the table in front of you at meetings, as it clearly indicates that your colleagues do not have your undivided attention and that's just rude

7. Using headphones in the office, perhaps because you are listening to music on your phone, should be avoided: you may argue that you are concentrating on your work, but it cuts you off from your colleagues and makes you look antisocial and inaccessible.

Social Media

Everyone can use their work computers to access social media, and – using the plethora of sites and platforms available – can maintain contact with friends throughout the working day. But a compulsive engagement with social media on the part of your employees should be discouraged. It is a huge distraction and, if employees integrate their private life so thoroughly into their work life, they are guilty of abusing the trust of their employers.

However, social media is here to stay, and it would be unwise to be too draconian about its use. Indeed, tech-savvy employees may actually bring benefits to the company. For many employers social media is a communication and networking tool and, as such, will have business applications that can be harnessed and exploited. Employees will inevitably be using social media. The important priority is to ensure that they use it well.

In addition, your company will probably have its own social media presence, with official accounts on a wide variety of platforms. You will need employees to administer these accounts, and build awareness of your company and brand amongst their own followers and networks. With good management, your employees may become social media ambassadors for your brand.

Remember also, that social media is a good way of communicating directly, and informally, with your employees, or eliciting feedback, brainstorming new products, seeking out new ideas.

> The personal life of every individual is based on secrecy, and perhaps it is partly for that reason that civilised man is so nervously anxious that personal privacy should be respected.
>
> Anton Chekov

The Line Between Public and Private

No matter how friendly and convivial the work environment is, it is always sensible to draw clear distinctions between private and public life, and this is more crucial than ever in the social media era.

It is a good idea for employees to review the privacy settings on all their social media accounts. In the real world of work and careers it is imperative to curate your own brand, and project a squeaky clean image.

Of course, you will in any case need to be guarded about your personal data and online privacy. But you should also be aware that if you do not activate your privacy settings, your life will be laid bare for all to see. It is a well-known fact that recruiters scour the social media of potential candidates, and this can set off alarm bells.

Dangerous areas are: political rants, pictures of substance abuse, provocative pictures. Also be aware that tagged photos, many of which were not posted by you, can still be seen on Facebook. If these images are really damning you can request the tag to be removed through Facebook, or ask the friend who posted the photo to take it down.

Online Snooping

In an online era how much privacy do you really have at work? If an employee uses his or her company's IT systems – whether in the office or on a work-issued laptop at home – this use is likely to be monitored, inevitably because of the prevalence of cyber-threats. Privacy on work-issued computers is not recognised: your entire web-browsing history, for example, is accessible to your employer (though whether they exploit this access is another matter). Employers can also access social media messages, chats and emails, and may do so to collect data about their workers' effectiveness. Remember that any office messenger service, such as Slack, can be monitored by your employer, so you should never use it for private chats.

Clearly this level of access can be corrosive, undermining employee trust, and therefore employers must tell employees if they're being monitored, and why. It is within an employer's rights to insist that equipment should not be used for personal matters within working hours, but in most businesses trust and flexibility will go a long way, ensuring that staff feel valued rather than disrespected.

CHAPTER 10

COMMUNICATIONS IN THE OFFICE

The secret of good communication is careful thought and planning and the establishment of good habits. Before you can communicate with others, you have to be able to communicate with yourself, which means remembering what has to be communicated, and how, and to whom.

It doesn't matter whether you retain this information on your computer, on your mobile phone, on paper, in a personal organiser or in your mind (though beware of forgetting it). What does matter is that you regularly review what you are doing and for whom your work has implications and, therefore, what you need to communicate.

And you have to remember that communication is by its very nature a two-way process. You have to be able to receive communications as well as send them. It's no good firing off emails to all and sundry if you're not going to take any notice of replies and responses to them. It's no good inviting comments if you don't read them or respond to them when necessary.

The Purpose of Communication

Every communication must have a clear purpose. In a busy working day, none of us has time to deal with unnecessary communications.

It is therefore imperative that the purpose should be clearly stated. You can signal your purpose by opening your communications with the phrase, 'The purpose of this note is to…'. At least in this way you will be able to assess if there really is a reason for sending the note.

> ELECTRIC COMMUNICATION WILL NEVER BE A SUBSTITUTE FOR THE FACE OF SOMEONE WHO WITH THEIR SOUL ENCOURAGES ANOTHER PERSON TO BE BRAVE AND TRUE.
> CHARLES DICKENS

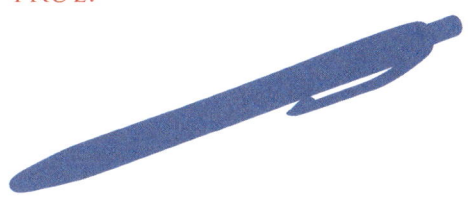

HALF OF THE WORLD IS COMPOSED OF PEOPLE WHO HAVE SOMETHING TO SAY AND CAN'T, AND THE OTHER HALF WHO HAVE NOTHING TO SAY AND KEEP ON SAYING IT.

ROBERT FROST

The Language of Communication

Here are a few points to consider:

1. Simple words and phrases are far more effective than complex ones.
2. Short sentences make sense.
3. Emotional language is seldom good business language.
4. 'Formal' doesn't mean 'long winded'.
5. Not everyone understands or appreciates jargon.
6. Written language should be kept as close as possible to spoken language.

The Blight of Jargon

The real problem with jargon is that it's anti-language and anti-communication. It's obfuscatory, rendering the simplest sentences opaque.

Never confuse jargon with expertise, and don't labour under the misapprehension that jargon will impress your colleagues with your grasp of the matter in hand. All too often jargon is used as a smokescreen, attempting to obscure laziness and incompetence. Sentences like 'let's all be proactive about the way we interface, give it some face-time, run it up the flagpole and kick the tyres, then come up with a value-proposition that really shows we're tasked with thinking the unthinkable…' are cliché-ridden and circumlocutory, communicating nothing.

Don't use jargon to over-complicate simple concepts, thinking it will make you look more professional. A sentence like 'let's get our ducks in a row, seek end-user perspective and keep Jamie in the loop' could easily be translated as 'let's get organised, consult the customers and keep Jamie informed'.

Don't assume that jargon will disguise ignorance or wrong-foot colleagues and clients, or obscure your own ineffectiveness. Think carefully about what you are trying to say. It is never a mistake to write, and speak, in plain, jargon-free English. You will be praised for the incisiveness of your thinking, and rewarded for your ability to communicate clearly.

Written or Spoken?

If you write something, normally by email, and send it, you know that you have fulfilled your part of the communication process. The rest is up to the recipient of the email/note etc. The value of a written communication is its permanency. Once it's in your email 'Sent' box, or on file, you can prove that you sent it. The person to whom the note was sent can't easily deny receiving it. The drawbacks of a written communication are that what's delivered cannot be disavowed, and there may be some delay in receiving feedback, although in business matters many of us would like time to think before we have to respond.

It is certainly true that wily operators within a business environment will be very aware that sending out emails, and copying in team members, is an effective way of covering your back. You are not only doing your job, you are seen to be doing so and you are demonstrating that you are an effective communicator.

Inevitably, however, there are some benefits to a spoken exchange. You can safely assume the message was received and digested, unless it is clear that the person you're talking to isn't listening. It should also be possible to get some idea of how your communication has been received and what response it provokes. This is where speech has the advantage over writing. But each has its place, its value and its pitfalls.

The value of spoken communication is that it's immediate, it's direct and it allows an instant response. It allows both sides to gauge how the other is feeling about the exchange, and modify their discussion of the original point accordingly. The drawbacks of spoken communications are that either side can deny that the conversation ever took place, or suggest that it covered a totally different subject, or be very selective in recalling what was said. There's also the risk that tempers may become frayed in the heat of the moment and that things are said which are later regretted.

> THE SINGLE BIGGEST PROBLEM IN
> COMMUNICATION IS THE ILLUSION
> THAT IT HAS TAKEN PLACE.
> GEORGE BERNARD SHAW

The following are bad mistakes when telling somebody something verbally:

- Choosing a time when the other person is busy dealing with something else.
- Delivering a private message in public.
- Trying to cram too much into one conversation.
- Adopting the wrong tone (eg hectoring when it should be persuasive).
- Turning a blind eye or a deaf ear to the reply.

Memos

Traditionally, these were printed on hard copy and circulated around the company. They were considered to be a good medium for passing on general information or congratulations to the members of the office or a specific department. Or they might be used as a succinct cover note on the top of a bundle of documents.

The vast majority of this kind of information would today be conveyed by email, although some offices may still choose to retain an 'internal memorandum' culture. If that is the case, keep memos short and informal, and send them out on plain, unheaded paper. Whether you are sending an email 'memo' (much more likely), or an old-fashioned memo, the basic style of presentation is the same:

TO: Sales Department
FROM: Charlotte Lessing
CC: John Berkeley
DATE: 7 July 2021
SUBJECT: Customer Presentation

The marketing presentation that you prepared last week to showcase our new product lines was absolutely excellent.

Your enthusiasm, creativity and product knowledge were very impressive, and certainly sealed the deal with ABC Enterprises.

Thank you for your work and dedication; a celebratory drink is in order, and I will let you know where and when.

My sincere congratulations.

When to Communicate?

It is a sad fact of life that we spend more time on the things that go wrong than on those that go right. We put pen to paper to complain more often than we do to praise. We believe we have to issue warnings and make complaints. We assume that we don't have to pass on praise.

All too often we don't do anything to show appreciation for hard work, high-performance, increased productivity. By failing to congratulate colleagues on their success, we are guilty of bad practice and bad manners.

Private vs Public Communication

Any communications that deal with an individual's shortcomings should be delivered to that individual directly, for his or her eyes only. If all is going well with one person or one department, however, there is no need to keep it a secret. By publicly praising one individual, you encourage (or maybe challenge) others. Be wary of overusing this technique. If the same person is acknowledged as flavour of the month from January to December, there is a good chance that others will lose hope or interest.

It is, of course, vital that all those entitled to recognition for a piece of good work get noticed. It is an error of the worst and most divisive order to communicate thanks and appreciation to A, B and C and leave out D. If that mistake is made, then it must be rectified as soon as possible, and an appropriate apology made.

Inviting others to communicate

As a matter of good sense and courtesy, it should be made clear in any workplace that comments and suggestions are invited from all who work there as to how practices could be improved. If you believe in any kind of office or workplace democracy, then you have to show that you are prepared to listen to the complaints and the proposals of colleagues and employees. Communication has to be a two-way process.

> The more we elaborate our means of communication, the less we communicate.
> J B Priestley

Once complaints or proposals have been made, you have to show that they are taken seriously. A communication from any member of staff must be acknowledged. If it cannot be dealt with at once, then the member of staff must be informed of this, and given some indication as to when it will be. One of the criteria by which a business is judged, from within and without, is how promptly, politely and efficiently it responds to the initiatives and the communications of others.

Asking Favours

If you wish to ask a favour of someone, unless it's a small request, or asked of a close colleague, it is usually fairer to communicate this in writing. Confronting someone face-to-face puts them on the spot. If they want to decline, but to do so politely and not cause offence, they have no time to produce an excuse that saves the face of both parties. It is also not good manners to preface any such request with 'I'm sure you won't mind…' or any similar phrase if the person says he or she can't help, it is impolite to ask why not, or to sweep aside the apology.

Turning down a request for help should be done as politely as possible. There is no need to go into elaborate explanations. However tempting it may be, it is not polite to rid yourself of the person making the request by suggesting the names of other people he or she could try, unless you genuinely believe these people may wish and be able to help.

Giving Sympathy

If a member of staff is taken ill and needs sick leave, it is good practice to send a letter or card to them showing concern and wishing them a quick recovery. The more serious the illness, the more important it is to write to them, but the more tactful the message needs to be.

If a close relative of a member of staff dies, then a note of condolence is appropriate. Who should send this note is a matter for the individual company, but it should come from a senior member of staff. Close colleagues of the bereaved person will almost certainly make their own gestures of sympathy. Choosing the right words isn't easy at such times, but time and trouble should be spent on this, as a personal message, however brief, will be greatly valued.

CHAPTER 11

TELEPHONE ETIQUETTE

A phone call often gives an outsider the first (and, perhaps the only) impression of an office, a department, or an entire company.

Every employee should try to cultivate a pleasant phone manner. People should be encouraged to speak clearly and to adopt certain basic phone practices – giving the company name and their own name or department – on answering the phone.

First Impressions

Picking up a phone when it rings and saying 'yes?' or 'what?' is not good manners and doesn't impress. Giving the name of the company or department in a voice that implies that the caller is a thorough nuisance and could not have picked a more inconvenient time to phone is clearly undesirable. Picking up the phone and continuing a conversation with someone else before deigning to speak to whoever is on the other end of the line is just rude.

The way you answer the phone reveals a great deal. It tells the caller something about the sort of people your company employs, but it may go much further than that. It will probably set the tone for the whole conversation – or at least profoundly influence it. The caller who is already in a bad mood will not be satisfied if your response is grudging or discourteous. A caller who is having difficulty obtaining information may well give up in disgust if you treat his or her call with bored disdain. A caller who has something to offer that may be of benefit to your company may also hang up if it sounds from your tone of voice that you couldn't care less.

At the very least, you should identify yourself and the company you represent, and speak clearly. If appropriate, a simple 'how can I help you?' will go a long way towards setting the right tone for your call.

THE DAY WILL COME WHEN THE MAN AT THE TELEPHONE WILL BE ABLE TO SEE THE DISTANT PERSON TO WHOM HE IS SPEAKING.

ALEXANDER GRAHAM BELL

Telephone Calls: The Ten Commandments

1. Try to make your voice sound clear and pleasant. It should convey that you are paying attention.

2. It helps if you smile in a friendly manner when you answer the phone. The caller can't see you, but your demeanour will be evident in your tone of voice, and you will sound much more welcoming.

3. You should identify who and what and possibly where you are at the moment you answer.

4. Listen carefully to what the caller has to say to you – it can be irritating to be asked to repeat information because someone has not been listening properly.

5. You should take special care in noting the name of the caller, the name of the person he or she wishes to speak to, and any other names that crop up during the conversation.

6. You should be patient and tolerant on the phone. If the caller has not sufficiently prepared what he or she has to say, then you have to give them a chance to make up for that.

7. If the caller has come through to the wrong extension, or the call isn't for you, then you shouldn't give the impression that you think it is the caller's fault – or anyone else's fault, for that matter.

8. If you have to interrupt the caller (for example to redirect them to someone who can be more helpful), then you should interrupt as politely as possible.

9. If you promise to leave somebody a message, you should do so right away, to avoid forgetting.

10. If you promise to call back, you should keep this promise.

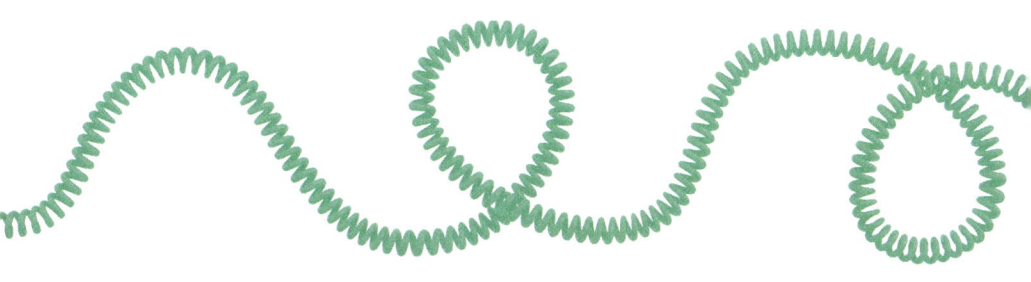

Telephone Lies

In almost all cases honesty is the best policy on the telephone, though the temptations to lie are enormous. A classic case is when you are acting as a buffer between the caller and someone within your office who may not wish to speak to the caller. Making a lame excuse like 'I don't think he/she is in the office right now' and then cupping your hand over the receiver and hissing 'it's Joe Bloggs – do you want to speak to him?' will make it perfectly apparent that you are vetting your colleague's calls.

If you need to find out if someone is available to speak, or to ask for advice or information, put the caller on hold, so you can speak without inhibitions. Do not rely on the ineffective hand over the receiver – it muffles the sound but snatches of conversation will still be audible.

It also isn't fair to inform the caller that you 'won't keep you one moment' if you know that there is going to be a long delay in taking the call. It's better to be truthful – waiting only makes people cross. If, however, you admit that there is going to be a long wait and suggest that you get someone at your end to call back, then you have to keep this promise.

Shunting calls to innocent colleagues simply because you don't want to have to deal with them is a shabby trick, unfair to caller and colleagues alike.

The only telephone lie that usually works is when you say 'I'm sorry, I'm afraid there is no one here at the moment who can help you…'. It works because the caller cannot prove that there is – whatever he or she may suspect. But it's a lie with a limited life, as the caller will either demand 'when will there be somebody there who can help?' or will ring back anyway.

> I LIKE TEXTING AS MUCH AS THE NEXT KIDULT – AND EMBRACE IT AS YET MORE EVIDENCE, ALONG WITH EMAIL, THAT WE LIVE NOW IN THE POST-AURAL AGE, WHEN AN UNSOLICITED PHONE CALL IS, THANKFULLY, BECOMING MORE AND MORE UNDERSTOOD TO BE AN UNSPEAKABLE SOCIAL SOLECISM, TANTAMOUNT TO AN IMPERTINENT INVASION OF PRIVACY.
> WILL SELF

Handling Unwanted Calls

Once it has become clear that you are dealing with an unwanted phone call, it's tempting to slam the receiver down or wickedly pass on the call to an unsuspecting colleague. Though very understandable, both courses of action should be avoided. Unwanted callers often ring back if cut off in full flow, and your poor colleagues will almost certainly guess who passed the call on.

Instead listen carefully to unwanted calls to establish if this is a call that should genuinely be put through to someone else. If not, you will have to attempt to bring the call to a speedy, but polite, end. The best policy is to say firmly, but politely: 'I'm so sorry, there really isn't anyone here who deals with problems of that nature' and then sign off with a general and genuine-sounding mutter of regret that you are unable to help.

Voicemail

This handy facility provides a 24/7 non-stop point of contact with the rest of the world. However, it can easily become a headache, especially when countless callers leave rambling messages, indecipherable numbers and pleas to call back.

Try and cut some of these problems off at the outset by recording a personalised voicemail message. This should contain the following information: your name/number/department (whatever you would normally use when answering your phone); a polite message along the lines of 'I'm afraid I can't come to the phone right now, but please leave your name and number and I'll call you back'. This should at least ensure that callers who leave a message are aware that they have reached the correct person, and it may even persuade them to keep their messages short and to the point.

Of course, this works both ways, and when you reach a voicemail in a business context, you should follow the same rules. Clearly state your name and number and ask to be called back (it helps if you state a time when you will be available). If necessary, you can add a very brief, succinct sentence about the nature of your business: 'I wonder if you could call me back about the sales projections for the first quarter'. This will alert the recipient to the information you require and will save time.

It is imperative that you call back message-leavers, and do so promptly.

Difficult Calls

From time to time tempers are lost in the world of business. Irascible telephone callers are not unknown, but no matter how grave the provocation, nobody should stoop to rudeness. If you are the victim of such behaviour, there are sadly no foolproof ways of dealing with rudeness on the telephone. Prevention is always better than cure, so the first thing you have to do is make sure that you are never the cause of invective or personal remarks. If the caller starts to be uncivil, then you are entitled to point this out to him or her, and this is probably the best thing to do. It's best not to do so snappily or waspishly, and never threateningly – there is nothing a bad-tempered caller likes better than the sniff of combat in the air.

Terminating The Call

If you've pointed out that you believe the caller is being rude and this hasn't calmed him or her down, then you are at liberty to tell the caller that you are (reluctantly) going to have to put the phone down, and that you hope that it will be possible to have a reasonable conversation at another time. You should then follow through on your threat and actually put the phone down – don't hang on to see what effect this has.

What you shouldn't do, no matter how much you'd like to, is pass the offending caller on to someone else. If the caller is making threats, however, or is being intimidating or offensive, then you should let your boss know, or at least look for support from a colleague once the call is over. If things get out of hand you may want to record the call, but you should always tell the caller you are going to do so.

Mobiles

We all have mobiles now, and some of us have dedicated business mobiles. It is inevitable that they will be used in a business context, and in most cases the same rules apply to mobiles as to business landlines.

If you're using your phone for work, record business contacts by name, so that you will see them on your incoming caller display, and will be able to greet them in a friendly and professional manner. Do not expect your recipient to have done the same; when they answer the phone, clearly state who you are.

If you know your mobile will be used by business contacts, make sure that you have a sensible and informative voicemail message.

If you are using your mobile when outside the office, for example to explain that you are going to be late for a meeting with a client, have the courtesy to find a quiet place to make the call. An inaudible communication, interrupted by station announcements or traffic noise, will cause irritation and communicate nothing.

You will inevitably use texts in a business context: sometimes it will be to simply tell someone that you are running late for a meeting, or to give them a meeting location; on other occasions you may be sending a brief message with substantial news. Bear in mind that texts are ideal for conveying short, instant messages. Important information may need a more lengthy and nuanced explanation; if in doubt, send an email where you have more flexibility and space.

If you are sending a text to someone you don't know, or to a business contact who may or may not have a record of your number, it is a good idea to include a sign-off at the end of your message – eg 'Thanks, Jessica'.

> YOU SHOULD NEVER GO TO A MEETING OR MAKE A TELEPHONE CALL WITHOUT A CLEAR IDEA OF WHAT YOU ARE TRYING TO ACHIEVE.
> STEVE JOBS

Email Communication

CHAPTER 12

Email has replaced many traditional forms of communication, including formal written business correspondence, telephone calls and informal verbal communications. Most internal office communications are now by email, although direct messaging systems, such as Slack, are becoming increasingly popular because communication is in real time and responses are immediate.

It must be remembered that email is digital, and messages may be stored permanently and propagated exponentially. There is no such thing as a secure or confidential email. It should not be used for delicate communications or anything that the sender would not want to be attributed to himself/herself.

Emails are extremely convenient and facilitate communication greatly, but do not let the ease of the medium encourage you to take short-cuts, use abbreviations, write non-sentences, or discard punctuation. As always, you must use emails to communicate clearly, so make it a rule to take a few minutes to pause and read what you have written.

Nothing replaces real paper and ink; email should not be used for formal correspondence, such as replying to postal invitations or sending thank-you letters. These rules also apply to social emails.

Subject Line and Importance Label

The subject line is a summary of the content of the email, and should alert the recipient. A well-written subject line will ensure that the message gets the appropriate attention. It may also expedite the response time; if the recipient sees a helpful subject line previewed in their email inbox they may prioritise replying. Bear in mind that it is also used for filing and retrieval purposes so it is important that it accurately reflects the topic of the email.

The 'importance' label should be used discriminatingly. Otherwise it will be ignored because of its frequent misuse.

CC AND BCC

Copies (cc) can be sent to individuals who only need to view the information for reference. They should be ordered alphabetically, or – in a business environment – by importance.

Blind copying (bcc) should be used with discernment; it is deceptive to the primary recipient. If possible, the email should be forwarded on to the third party, with a short note explaining any confidentiality, after its distribution.

If blind copying is essential – ie for a confidential document where all recipients must remain anonymous – then senders should address the email to themselves, and everyone else as 'bcc' recipients.

If an email is being sent to a small group, it is acceptable to use the 'To' and 'cc' fields. If the email is being used to communicate with entire departments, it is best to create a group, a facility that is available in most email programmes, and give it a name such as 'The Sales Team', or 'The Design & Editorial Team'.

Think carefully before you copy people in to your email correspondence. We're all in danger of being swamped by digital communication and your contributions to the deluge may not be appreciated.

PUNCTUATION AND LANGUAGE

Don't be bamboozled by the digital medium into over-using slang and jargon and under-using punctuation. Write in short, clear sentences.

Ensure that correct punctuation is used. Do not use lower case letters throughout as this can appear lazy. Capital letters, on the other hand, may look over-insistent. If you want to emphasise something, try underlining or using italics.

Avoid abbreviations and text language. Many recipients will find this irritating or incomprehensible.

Email is a conversational medium, but this should not be reinforced by over-punctuating. Exclamation marks can look somewhat hectic and over-emphatic, emojis may appear childish and kisses should be avoided in a business context, where you need to be projecting calm professionalism.

It is exhausting knowing that most of the time the phone rings, most of the time there's an email, most of the time there's a letter, someone wants something of you.

Stephen Fry

Reply vs Reply All

Pause before you hit the 'reply all' button. Your colleagues may be very frustrated if they are inundated with all sorts of irrelevant correspondence. On the other hand, hitting 'reply' and thereby excluding some salient individuals is also bad etiquette.

It is also always a good idea to stop and think for a few moments before actually hitting the 'Send' button.

Salutations and Sign-Offs

Retain the same level of formality that you would use in all correspondence (eg 'Dear Sir', 'Dear Mr Brown', 'Dear Bob'). If you're approached with informality, then reciprocate in kind.

In formal emails you might use 'Yours faithfully/sincerely'; in the vast majority of cases you'll use something more casual (eg 'Best wishes'). In a business context, it's always useful to add your full name, job title and telephone number under your sign-off. Many companies like their employees to use a pre-designed 'footer' with the company logo, as well as your personal title and contact details.

Internal emails will depend on the office culture. The salutation and sign-off will be less formal than written letters: 'Hi Sarah' and 'Best wishes' may be perfectly acceptable for a colleague.

Always bear in mind that an email 'trail' might become relevant to other employees at some point, so resist the temptation to add emojis, slang and nicknames.

Threads and Attachments

Maintain threads (all the previous emails on a subject) where appropriate. If a long thread is to be retained, bear in mind that a pithy 'I agree' isn't very helpful – you may need to briefly summarise what you agree with, which will save your colleagues having to scroll through reams of correspondence.

Always read back through the previous threads to check that nothing has been said that the recipient(s) should not read.

If your email is the last entry in an ever-lengthening and daunting thread, discard it if at all possible and start anew – your colleagues will appreciate the fresh slate approach.

Be discriminating about overloading emails with system-slowing extras. Always send a covering note with attachments.

Responding to Emails

The important thing about email communication in the office is to keep on top of it. Don't let that little notification number on your email icon clock up. Try to answer emails as they come in, or set aside regular times during the day when you clear the backlog.

At the same time, you should bear in mind the immediacy with which you can reply to an email, and always take extra care and pause for thought. Sending an intemperate 'flaming' email (replete with offensive language, sarcasm, insults and hostility) may be a mistake from which you will not recover.

If you don't have time to reply fully (and temperately), send a holding email, something along the lines of 'This looks really interesting. I will be reviewing it in more detail over the next couple of days and will get back to you on Friday' (and make a note to reply when you say you will).

The most important thing is to be responsive – nobody wants to feel that their communications are falling into a black hole.

Business Correspondence

CHAPTER 13

While a vast amount of correspondence is now conducted by email, rules of presentation, grammar and formality still apply. Despite the ease of email communication there is still a place for formal business letters, well presented on headed notepaper, and laid out according to long-observed conventions. The physical object confers a certain gravitas to the communication, and for that reason letters are often used for agreements, orders, confirmation of employment, formal warnings, and so on.

Additional stationery items, such as compliments slips and business cards, are also very useful in the carefully calibrated world of business correspondence and communication.

The Art of Letter Writing

The purpose of business letter writing (as of all other forms of correspondence) is to relay or solicit information in the clearest, shortest and most relevant way. The first question to be answered is 'is this letter necessary?'. If it isn't, you shouldn't send it. The second question is 'what sort of paper is appropriate?' There is no point in using an A4 sheet of headed notepaper if the letter consists of a single sentence.

Finally you should consider whether a handwritten letter is appropriate – this might be a good idea if you are conveying thanks, or congratulations, as it clearly adds a personal touch. But beware; if your handwriting is inelegant or illegible, a handwritten letter will be a source of frustration, not gratification.

> The word that is heard perishes, but the letter that is written remains.
>
> Latin proverb

THE MOST VALUABLE OF ALL TALENTS IS THAT OF NEVER USING TWO WORDS WHEN ONE WILL DO.

Thomas Jefferson

Salutation Considerations

This can be a matter of concern when commencing a business letter. Do you put 'Dear John'? Or should it be 'Dear Mr Debrett'? It is becoming increasingly acceptable to put 'Dear John Debrett' instead, if you are writing to someone you have not met. To use the first name and family name is less formal and less impersonal than using 'Mr' or 'Ms' and the surname, but isn't crudely over-friendly. It also deals with the difficult question of whether to address a female recipient as 'Ms', 'Miss' (old-fashioned, but preferred by some individuals), or 'Mrs'.

Once you have met the addressee, or once you have already exchanged letters, or if the correspondence has been initiated by 'John' addressing you by your first name, then you can drop the family name.

If you don't know to whom you should address the letter (eg if it is of a speculative nature or if it's a letter of complaint), then the best thing to do is telephone the company concerned and find out. It is still acceptable to head letters 'Dear Sir/Madam', but it suggests that you haven't taken the trouble to find out whom you are writing to, and are forced to take resource to a very old fashioned salutation.

Sign-Offs

The way you begin the letter will dictate how you sign off. The old conventions still apply here. If you have started the letter with 'Dear Sir' or 'Dear Madam', then you should end with 'yours faithfully'. If you have started with 'Dear Ms Vaughan' or 'Dear Amy Vaughan', then you should end with 'yours sincerely' and sign with your full name. If you opened with 'Dear John' or 'Dear Caroline', then you should use 'yours sincerely' and sign the letter with just your first name, though you should type your forename and surname below the signature.

Often PAs or secretaries sign letters for their bosses, inserting the letters 'pp' before their own signature, but retaining the name of the boss (and nominated letter-writer) below the signature. The letters 'pp' stand for the Latin words *per procurationem*, which means 'on behalf of'. This practice usually indicates that the boss was out of the office when the time came to sign the letter, and that the PA or secretary has the total trust of his or her boss. However, the more awesome, the more dignified, the more powerful the addressee, the more it behoves the boss to sign the letter personally.

Replying to letters

Junk mail needs no response. Unsolicited mail in general may have to wait its turn for an answer, but it is still considered bad manners by most people if you do not reply to your mail. If you wish to make a phone call or send an email instead of writing a letter, that is perfectly acceptable in most cases. Where you need particularly to acknowledge an order, contract, or complaint, then a letter should be sent. In general terms, the sooner the letter is written and sent, the better. There are many who judge a company and its staff by the speed and efficiency with which they deal with their mail.

Business Letters Summary

Business letters should be printed on A4 paper that features the sender's company logo, postal address, telephone number and email address, and company number and VAT number where required.

Recipient's Address and Date

This can be ranged left for a clean, modern look, although in some companies the preference is to range the address right. The address will contain the following information: the recipient's title (Mr, Mrs, Ms, Dr, Professor, Lord, Sir etc), the recipient's business title, eg Sales Director, Training Manager etc, the recipient's company name in full, the address and postcode.

The date goes underneath the recipient's name and address. Leave a minimum of one line space before the date. The recommended British style is '15 July 2021', but house styles may vary. Consistency is important.

Subject Line

This should be a brief informative line that will help with filing and clarity. It might mention a reference number in response to an earlier letter. It is placed (centred or ranged left) under the salutation. Leave one line space above and below the subject line, before the body of the letter.

Format

Letters are typed with two spaces after a full stop, one space after a comma. This style does not apply to longer text documents, such as company reports. It is advisable to keep business letters concise, to the point and preferably on one side of a sheet of A4 paper.

Signatures

Always try to sign letters by hand whenever possible. An electronic signature is just about acceptable for a mass marketing mailshot or similar, but looks careless if it is used in direct correspondence.

The sender's name, in full, is added, with the job title on the line below, underneath the space allocated for the signature. If the letter has opened with the recipient's forename only ('Dear John'), then it should be signed with just a forename, but you should still ensure that the sender's full name and job title is included under the signature.

The inclusion of the sender's title in brackets after the sender's name – for example 'Eliza Curzon (Miss)' – is becoming a less-used tradition. It is, however, helpful as it provides the recipient with the correct form of address for the reply letter.

Final Notations

These are traditional notations, which are disappearing from contemporary correspondence. For example, the initials of the person who typed the letter may be added, or the abbreviation 'encl.' to indicate that an enclosure is included with the letter. If the letter is being circulated, the initials 'cc' can be added, with an alphabetical list of all the recipients. Notations are separated with a forward slash.

Envelopes

Since envelopes are now no longer individually typed, it is acceptable to use adhesive labels for substantial mailouts.

It is preferable to handwrite addresses on envelopes when sending out important correspondence. Window envelopes are only really appropriate for mass mail-outs or invoices.

When to Use Headed Notepaper

Business letters should always be sent on company notepaper. Company headed paper should not, however, be used for the following:

- Letters of a personal nature. This is a difficult area to define. Often you write letters of congratulation or condolence both as a private individual and as a representative of the company for whom you work. In such cases, company paper is appropriate. If you are writing purely as a private individual, however, you should use private paper.

- Any letters that express private opinions – eg political views. To link your company with a party political opinion or policy is a breach of business etiquette. This rule also applies to letters that seek to raise funds for charities, unless the fundraising is sponsored by your company and has been carried out in their name.

- Letters which express views and opinions markedly different from those of your company.

- Letters of an application for jobs with other companies. It is simply a matter of courtesy to the company for which you work not to use its headed notepaper for this purpose. If you are seen to be discourteous to your present employer, a potential future employer may have doubts about you.

- Letters to the media about your job or your company or related topics that express personal opinions.

- Any letters that don't relate to company matters.

Second Thoughts

For every piece of work there is a deadline, and that means pressure to get matters dealt with quickly. Occasionally there are letters or emails that require extra thought. Second thoughts are best applied to business letters written in anger. If you have sent a letter, and subsequently wish you hadn't, then the only thing you can do is to contact the person to whom you sent the letter, explain how you now feel and offer whatever apology you wish to make.

Before sending the letter of complaint, it's a good idea to sit back and take stock of the situation that has prompted the wish to complain. Ponder the following questions:

1. Is it appropriate to complain about this matter? On reflection, do you still feel that the complaint is warranted?

2. What sort of complaint should be made? (eg for recompense? for an apology?).

3. Is the complaint actually justified – or are you being over-sensitive? It is a good idea to solicit other people's opinions on this matter.

4. Are you making the complaint to the right person? If you are unsure, you can always phone the company in question to obtain the right name.

5. Are you looking for a solution to a problem? Or are you simply looking for a fight?

6. Are there colleagues or bosses with whom you should consult before making this complaint?

If you're uncertain about any of these points, then it's time for second thoughts. This may be a letter that should not be sent.

> THIS AT LEAST SHOULD BE A RULE THROUGH THE LETTER-WRITING WORLD: THAT NO ANGRY LETTER BE POSTED TILL FOUR-AND-TWENTY HOURS WILL HAVE ELAPSED SINCE IT WAS WRITTEN.
> ANTHONY TROLLOPE

Compliments Slips

A compliments slip contains the same information that would appear on the standard company letterhead, and is pre-printed with the words 'With compliments'. Usually, these are designed to fit, unfolded, into a standard DL business envelope. A short handwritten note and signature can be added.

Compliments slips are a convenient shorthand enclosure to attach to, for example, a cheque, or a catalogue or price list that has been requested by a customer. They can be a pleasing addition to a routine mail-out and a way of maintaining good public relations.

They should never be used as a substitute for a handwritten note, and there are many occasions on which a compliments slip is not adequate – for example when you are sending thanks for help or hospitality, or posting a personal package. On these occasions a handwritten note on headed writing paper is always preferable.

Some companies choose to use A5 headed writing paper, or an A5 card, which serves the same function as a compliments slip or can be used for sending out brief handwritten notes.

Faxes

Faxes are much less prevalent in the era of email communication, but many companies still have fax machines, which double up as printers and photocopiers. It should be noted that a fax is legally seen as a method of serving a notice, so faxes should never be dismissed as unimportant.

The cover sheet should include the following essential information: recipient's name, company name and fax number; sender's name, company name, telephone number and fax number. A brief explanation and indication of the number of pages can also be helpful.

BUSINESS CARDS

These are used primarily for professional or business purposes, but with the decline of the visiting card they have taken on some of its social functions. Social usage should, however, be infrequent. Cards are usually printed, but may be engraved if a smarter impression is thought appropriate.

Business cards are usually about the same size as a credit card and landscape in format (vertical layouts can look striking, but may be inconvenient for recipients' filing systems or cardholders). They should fit into a cardholder or the card section of a wallet. They should contain the following: the employee's name, without any prefixes (unless they have professional relevance, eg 'Professor'); the company's full postal address and website address; the company's landline number. The employee's direct line or mobile telephone number may also be included as well as the employee's email address.

On a standard business card, the name and professional title should be centred, in large characters, above the name of the firm, or below the company logo. The address, telephone, fax and email information should appear in smaller characters in the bottom left- and right-hand corners, or spread across the bottom.

On a business card that is intended to show the bearer's qualifications, the appropriate professional letters may be suffixed to the name, for example FRIBA. First degrees, for example BA (Hons), should not be included.

Reports and reviews

CHAPTER 14

Many companies have adopted a policy of conducting an annual (or perhaps more frequent) review of individual members of staff. The purpose of this is to make sure the subject's career is structured and that the best possible use is made of his or her talents. It is also a very effective way of keeping employees on their toes.

In general, certain guidelines should be available, and both reviewer or review board and subject should know the structure that is supposed to exist and should stick to it.

Managers should spend some time preparing for the review process. Enlist feedback from colleagues beforehand, and look over any notes you have made over the preceding months. Ensure that you know where you stand in relation to promotion and pay rises, so that you are not blindsided.

Advice for the Subject

1. You have to be prepared to be able to give a reasonable account of your performance. You have to be ready to justify your past or present salary and your future existence within the company.

2. You have to present yourself in the best possible light, and that includes dressing appropriately.

3. You have to be punctual.

4. You should know your rights. If there are rules governing the conduct of such reviews, you should be aware of them, especially in relation to any rights of appeal against the decision of the reviewer or review board.

> **Ordinary people think merely of spending time, great people think of using it.**
> Arthur Schopenhauer

WE ALL NEED
PEOPLE WHO
WILL GIVE US
FEEDBACK.
THAT'S HOW
WE IMPROVE.

BILL GATES

Advice for the Reviewer/Review Board

1. Ensure that there has been scrupulous adherence to the rules governing such reviews.

2. No matter how disappointing the subject's performance is believed to have been throughout the period under review, he or she must be allowed a fair hearing.

3. The purpose of any review or report should be to raise the level of the performance of the person or department in question.

4. Criticisms should always be justifiable – it's not permissible to hurl the odd extra jibe out of spite or because it's probably well deserved. Criticism should, of course, always be constructive.

5. Criticisms or condemnations uttered in a civil manner often have a devastating effect, crushing any desire on the recipient's part to answer back or request special consideration.

If a review or report leads to subsequent arguments and recriminations, then there should be a set procedure to deal with these. Matters can get out of hand when an insufficient framework exists to deal with the emotional backlash that can follow an unflattering report.

The main purpose of any review should be to locate good performance, encourage further effort, increase an individual's feeling of self-confidence and self-motivation, and identify what, if anything, is going wrong. Once identified, the important thing is then to present whatever is going wrong as a problem to which everybody is seeking the solution. Sitting down and discussing strategies with the subject will make them feel part of the process and they will be more invested in the outcome.

> CRITICISM MAY NOT BE AGREEABLE, BUT IT IS NECESSARY. IT FULFILS THE SAME FUNCTION AS PAIN IN THE HUMAN BODY. IT CALLS ATTENTION TO AN UNHEALTHY STATE OF THINGS.
> WINSTON CHURCHILL

Written Reports

It should always be clear who or what a written report is about, who compiled it, and to whom it is aimed. Care should be taken to see that everyone who is entitled to a copy of such a report receives it. This is as much a matter of business efficiency as it is of business etiquette. It is a good idea to compile a list of such people against which to check the dispatch of any report.

Like any other communication within office life, reports should be written with a desire to communicate rather than obfuscate information. No matter how glossy the presentation, a report stands or falls by the language in which it is written, and that should be as clear as possible.

Staying Positive

If you are conducing a review and you have criticisms or concerns about your employee, they will be much more palatable if they are bracketed by approbation and encouragement, both at the beginning and end of the review (whether it is written or verbal). If you do feel that criticism is called for, be honest and explicit about your employee's shortcomings; you do not want them to feel confused at the end of the proceedings, which is often the result when the reviewer attempts to ameliorate the impact of criticism with kind words.

It is important to make time and space to discuss your employees' career development. Ask them if they're happy in their work, quiz them about their hopes for the future, and establish whether they have any requests – such as training or specific work experience – that you can fulfil. Listen carefully to their responses, and remember that reviews and reports are not just about your own agenda, they're also about listening to your employees' concerns.

See Dismissals and Redundancies pp 147–49

Making Each Review Count

In companies where the entire staff is given an annual review, it has to be remembered that this same staff will all get together and compare notes about their own reviews. If the same criticisms are levelled at everyone, out of an understandable desire to raise all-round performance, then that criticism will lose much of its sting. If it seems that every report is the same report, and that only the name at the top has been changed, then praise doesn't seem like real praise, and adverse comment will seem like generalised tetchiness. The former will lead to resentment; the latter allows those who have been justifiably criticised to wriggle off the hook, as far as their own consciences are concerned.

Fatal Reports

If a report concludes that a certain employee should be dismissed, then good business etiquette decrees that they should be given this distressing news face to face. They should not learn of it by opening a letter. The temptation to hide behind a curt little note may be enormous, and your interview with them, at which they learn of their dismissal, may be uncomfortable in the extreme, but the professional fate of employees warrants more than a line or two in print. If you achieve a reputation for mail-order sacking, then you will almost certainly set up an office atmosphere where every envelope is seen as a potential letterbomb, and your employees are filled with nervous dread.

If your review procedures have been correctly followed, news of dismissal should not come as an overwhelming surprise. Keep the actual final interview short, and get straight to the point, without prevarication.

> The improvement of understanding is for two ends: first, our own increase of knowledge; secondly, to enable us to deliver that knowledge to others.
> John Locke

CHAPTER 15

Problem-Solving Procedures

It is one of the hard facts of business life that what is politic comes before what is polite. This doesn't mean that the niceties of etiquette have no place in dealing with complaints, however. In fact, your chances of weathering any legal storm or emerging victorious from any legal tussle are much increased if you adopt a civil approach to your adversaries. However nit-picking a complaint, you have to listen to it, assure the complainant that you will look into it, and then deal with it. In the tough world of business, everyone should be encouraged by the fact that there are times when what makes legal sense also makes social sense.

Complaints from Third Parties

Although you may appraise a person's work by how well they perform, by what goes right, you often tend to judge a person's worth by how they respond when things go wrong. A great deal of time is spent in any office dealing with complaints, and anyone who can do this well is worthy of respect as well as a good salary.

A wise company will always value the employee who can keep cool in the face of someone with a real grievance. The response to anyone making a complaint, however trivial, should always be positive. A negative reaction to a complaint only feeds bad feeling.

No matter how unwelcome the complaint is, it is always courteous to thank the complainant for pointing out the company's shortcomings and to say that you are sorry that there has been a problem – this is simply good manners. Never adopt a defensive or pugnacious stance; assume that the grievance is legitimate and listen carefully to the facts before responding. Ensure that, once the nature of the complaint has been understood, your response addresses the actual substance of the complaint. Compensatory gestures that do not touch on the real problem will be seen as inadequate.

> I THINK A COMPLIMENT OUGHT ALWAYS TO PRECEDE A COMPLAINT, WHERE ONE IS POSSIBLE, BECAUSE IT SOFTENS RESENTMENT AND INSURES FOR THE COMPLAINT A COURTEOUS AND GENTLE RECEPTION.
> Mark Twain

Incoming Complaints

Whoever the complaint comes from, the same rules should apply:

1. Make it apparent, from the initial response to the complaint, that there is a genuine desire to help.

2. Don't shunt complaints around, passing them on to someone else simply because the complainant is a pain in the neck or dealing with the complaint is going to involve a considerable amount of work.

3. Don't be afraid to call in higher authority if things are getting tricky.

4. Don't drop colleagues in it by saying (or suggesting) to the complainant that it's 'their fault'.

5. Don't make promises that can't be kept simply to mollify the complainant.

6. Take the time and trouble to understand exactly what the complaint consists of – not always easy if the complainant is in a foul temper.

7. Don't make any soothing offers that may be interpreted as attempts at bribery – you will only antagonise the complainant.

8. Stick rigidly to the established company policy when dealing with complainant.

Outgoing Complaints

Making a complaint to another organisation, as a customer or client, is a different matter. If you are making the complaint, then the first decision you have to make is whether you are going to complain in person, on the phone, by email or by letter. Turning up in person has its disadvantages. Arriving on the doorstep unheralded and uninvited may appear rude, and rudeness doesn't help your case.

Telephoning has its advantages and disadvantages. It certainly can't be considered rude, and an unexpected phone call can elicit a great deal of useful information about the company's attitude to your complaint.

A careful note should be made of whom you have spoken to, their position in the company, and of any action that they have promised to take. Alternatively, you can record the conversation, in which case it is polite to inform the people to whom you are speaking that this is what you are doing. A complaint made on the phone should be followed up by email or letter.

An email is a useful strategy; it allows you to set down your thoughts in writing, and to give careful consideration to the complaint you are making. But emails are all too easily ignored. You might, therefore, consider making a formal complaint in writing, and even send it by recorded delivery to ensure it is delivered. Unfortunately, at this point you have to wait for a reply, and that is entirely in the hands of the other side. Sometimes a combination of methods is best – send an email or letter, promising a follow-up phone call a week later, for example. That phone call must then be made.

With all complaints, it is essential to keep a record of what is said, to whom, by whom; what action is promised, when; what you say and what they say. You should never threaten any action that you don't intend to take. You should never be rude, despite provocation, and if the other side is rude, you should point this out and contrast it with your own good manners. You should always ask to whom you are speaking, and when on the phone, note to whom you are being referred. It all takes a great deal of time, but in the long run it's worth it once you get satisfaction.

A PROBLEM IS A CHANCE FOR YOU TO DO YOUR BEST.
DUKE ELLINGTON

Complaints from Within the Office

It is always a good idea to have a known and established machinery for dealing with in-house complaints (a person to whom the complaint should be made, a committee that sits to hear complaints, an accepted practice of bringing both sides to the complaint together, etc). This often helps to stop matters getting out of hand for several reasons:

- The matter will be handled by someone with experience in dealing with complaints.

- Any argument as to how the complaint should be handled (or by whom) will be circumvented.

- Both sides in what is, to all intents and purposes, a dispute, will have some idea of what to expect.

- Any ultimate decision appears to be a less personal matter – ie it doesn't look as if management sided with one party against the other from the start.

> WHEN COMPLAINTS ARE FREELY HEARD, DEEPLY CONSIDERED AND SPEEDILY REFORMED, THEN IS THE UTMOST BOUND OF CIVIL LIBERTY ATTAINED THAT WISE MEN LOOK FOR.
> JOHN MILTON

Dealing with Complaints: Basic Principles

Whether there are established protocols within the office or not, certain basic principles apply in dealing with any complaint:

1. A pleasant manner and an apparently sympathetic approach are always helpful.

2. The sooner an attempt is made to handle a complaint, the better.

3. Approaching the matter as though there is a problem here, and the aim of all concerned is to solve that problem, lessens the risk of a legacy of bitter personal animosity, either between the two sides to the dispute or between the 'loser' and the company itself.

4. Every opportunity should be given to the two sides to find their own acceptable solution to the problem (as long as the solution is compatible with office discipline).

5. People who complain should not automatically be regarded as troublemakers. There is such a thing as a justified complaint.

6. A complaint should always be dealt with at the most modest level possible – don't bring in the company solicitor to deal with the wrangle over who should park where in the office carpark.

7. The imposition of discipline should not be seen as an exercise in power.

8. If two people have been asked to work together and they are incompatible, something has to be done about it.

In the case of an internal complaint in an office, you are really dealing with a three-party issue: the complainant, the person complained of, and the company itself. Each party has obligations. Each party should know how to behave. Most internal complaints within an office fall into one of two categories: performance and attitude. Performance complaints relate to punctuality, not doing the job properly, passing work unfairly on to others, leaving early, spending too long over lunch etc. Behavioural complaints relate to how a person is treating his or her colleagues – showing too little respect, taking people for granted, being rude. At the most troubling end of the attitude spectrum are complaints about bullying and sexual harassment.

Making an Informal Complaint

If you wish to make an in-house complaint (about someone or something within the office), then you should follow any procedure that is laid down. Where there is no such ready-made structure, then you have to invent your own. Most in-house complaints concern people rather than procedures – a colleague is habitually rude, sexist, racist, late, or even sloppy and unhygienic.

The best approach here is the direct and informal approach. Explain to your colleague just what it is that he or she is doing that is causing upset. This should be done in the spirit of 'I'm sorry to have to bring this to your attention…', or 'I'm sure you haven't realised it but…', or 'I wonder if you would mind…'. The impression given should be that there is a problem and you are looking and hoping for a solution – not that you are out to cause trouble. That is why it's always best to make the complaint as soon as you are aware of the problem. If you put off complaining, there's always a risk that you will eventually over-react, or become strident and inarticulate.

It's best to confront problems head-on, rather than resorting to passive-aggressive techniques of getting the message across. Many offenders are too stupid to understand the point that is being made, or think that you're being playful, rather than deadly serious.

If the direct and informal approach doesn't work then you have to try other methods. If you look around, you may well find allies, and it's more than likely that others are as annoyed as you are. Elicit their help, and you may find that you can get the point across together. If all your attempts fail, you will have to decide whether your grievance warrants being escalated, and the next step is taking it to a manager.

There are times when the direct and informal approach doesn't work or is inappropriate. This is certainly the case when you are being victimised or bullied. At such times you have to consider what more formal methods are available to you.

> **To hear complaints with patience, even when complaints are vain, is one of the duties of friendship.**
> Samuel Johnson

Making a Formal Complaint

A complaint about a colleague should be made to the right person and in the right way. Unless there are good reasons not to, it is best to let the culprit know that you are going to make a formal complaint, and why. It gives the culprit a chance to make an eleventh-hour improvement or at least to offer some kind of apology and make a promise to do better in future. If, however, there is no improvement and the promise turns out to be an empty one, then the culprit cannot say that he or she hasn't had a fair warning.

Once you have said that you are going to make the complaint, you should go through with it. Although it's very understandable that you should make a complaint when you are angry, you should try to do so coherently and with all signs that your patience has finally been exhausted and you have been forced to take this reluctant action. Don't impetuously race off to your line manager, screaming and thumping desks. It is better to bite your tongue in the short term and make an appointment to see the manager (or whoever deals with internal complaints) at a convenient time. You will then be able to prepare your words carefully.

If the manager (or whichever third-party will be hearing the complaint) decides that the complaint should be made in front of the culprit, you should agree to that plan – unless you have very good reasons otherwise and are prepared to explain what those reasons are. It will be up to the third-party to make sure the hearing doesn't get out of hand. Again, the important points to remember are to make the complaint reasonably, to avoid getting into a slanging match, to be specific as to what you are complaining about and to adopt a generous (or at least reasonable) attitude to any proposed solution to the problem.

Obviously, if you know of other colleagues who have been similarly upset or annoyed by the culprit, it is a good idea to ask them if they, too, would like to make a formal complaint. Take care that you don't appear to be trying to stir up antagonism towards the culprit where none exists. This is a matter for careful thinking and considerable tact. In general, however, a complaint made by several people is treated more seriously than that made by a single individual. It is a good idea to make a note of any similar grievances that others expressed towards the culprit. This makes it much harder for those others to withdraw their support at the last moment.

Giving Criticism

It is essential to bear in mind that all criticism, positive or negative, should have only one aim – to improve whatever weakness or fault or bad behaviour is apparent in the person being criticised. Without such an aim, criticism degenerates into a wholly destructive force that will create an unpleasant atmosphere in the office for everyone who works there.

This means that criticism should always be specific – just who and what are being criticised must be clear. It's no good telling people that they do everything wrong, that they are totally inept. A criticism should highlight one aspect of their work or behaviour. No matter how bad they are, they can improve only one step at a time. Tell someone he or she is worthless and they won't know where to start trying to improve.

However it is voiced, all criticism must be justified. Specific examples of what is going wrong should be cited to whoever is being criticised, to help them focus on what they are doing wrong. In some instances, evidence will need to be produced, or a flat denial of wrongdoing cannot be refuted. Any such evidence should be produced calmly and reasonably; you do not want to make the offender feel that they are being subjected to a programme of persecution.

It is acceptable to delegate to others the task of voicing a criticism where it would be overwhelming if the criticism came from, for example, the managing director but would sound weighty but not crippling if it came from, say, the head of department. It's always possible to turn to someone in higher authority if the person criticised does nothing to improve matters. However, handing over the task of making the criticism to another always runs the risk of that criticism being poorly expressed, or unfocused, or lacking the weight of personal experience.

Taking Criticism

The immediate unnatural and childish reaction to most criticism is to reject it. Even if the criticism is totally unjustified, however, and your indignation is entirely understandable, you should not lose your temper. If you wish to set out to prove that you are being wrongly appraised, then you will need a cool head and calm nerves. An intemperate reaction will do little to establish yourself in the eyes of others as the sort of reliable, conscientious member of the team who would never put a foot wrong.

If the criticism is justified, then you have to accept it with as good grace as possible. None of us likes having our faults listed, but none of us is perfect and we all do have faults. It is best to assume that the criticism comes with the best motives, rather than taking refuge in the paranoid assumption that your critic is out to get you, or score points. If the criticism is made in an unfair way, however, or at the wrong time, or in front of the wrong people, then you may rightly point this out.

Once a colleague or someone in authority has pointed out what you are doing wrong, then the next step is largely up to you. If you can't remedy the situation without the help of others, then you must ask for that help. If the solution lies entirely in your hands, then you should acknowledge this and take the necessary steps. If there is no solution to the problem, then you have to explain the situation and ask for understanding and tolerance. Above all, see the criticism as a way of helping you do better, and thank the person who has criticised you for their constructive feedback

If the criticism is unjustified, then you need to point this out immediately. Try not to sound defensive, and ensure that you tell the right person at the right time in the right way, for what you are really doing in not accepting the criticism, is making a criticism yourself.

WE CAN COMPLAIN BECAUSE ROSE BUSHES HAVE THORNS, OR REJOICE BECAUSE THORN BUSHES HAVE ROSES.

Abraham Lincoln

Dismissals and Redundancies

It's a sad day for everyone concerned when someone has to be sacked, or made redundant, but that doesn't mean that all pretence of good manners should go by the board. A person who is being 'let go' is entitled to decent treatment. News of dismissal should be communicated by whoever is responsible, in private, face-to-face with the person being concerned. Certain points may be helpful:

1. Sacking someone, or making them redundant, should be done humanely, without any blustering or bitter recriminations.

2. A clear reason should be given for the dismissal.

3. If whoever is being let go starts to argue, then the person in authority should try to avoid being drawn into that argument – it will only deteriorate into a row.

4. Letting an employee go should appear to be done more in sorrow than in anger.

5. It is best to keep the interview as short as possible. This is no time to start discussions on redundancy terms – better to allow the person who is being dismissed to swallow the bad news and beat a hasty retreat.

6. On the other hand, it may be an appropriate moment to express general support or sympathy, or at least thank the person being dismissed or made redundant for their contribution to the company's progress (no irony or sarcasm under any circumstances).

7. If the person who is being let go expresses a wish that they would prefer news of their departure to be kept quiet, this should be respected as far as possible.

8. If someone is to be let go, they should be informed of this as soon as possible to suppress rumours and speculation.

News of dismissal or redundancy should be conveyed in person, and only by note or letter (never by email or phone) if it is absolutely impossible to find somebody to deliver the news. It's bad manners to give someone notice of their imminent departure in this surreptitious way, and dismissing someone in person means that you can verify that they have fully understood what has happened and why.

Marching Orders

It has increasingly become the practice to sack people or make them redundant and order them to clear their desks and be gone on the same day. In some cases management have deemed it necessary to have the person escorted from the premises, and we are all familiar with the spectacle of dismissed workers leaving the building, carrying poignant boxes of possessions. This is a sad reflection of the new pragmatism: it is desirable to clear superfluous people out as soon as possible and to safeguard the company against the danger that they will walk out with crucial information about clients and contracts. Nevertheless, the tendency to insist on a peremptory departure shows little regard for their dignity or appreciation of their worth.

Leaving a job, especially unwillingly, can be one of the most traumatic things that can happen to anyone. Depriving that person of the chance to say a proper goodbye to colleagues and work is as unkind as it is ill mannered. Such practices also breed fear in the rest of the workforce, and fear is never a good motivator.

Given that such crude practices exist, however, the least that the rest of us can do is to help those in distress. If someone has been sacked and ordered to clear their desk immediately, then offer to lend a hand.

You may assist in clearing out a desk or filing cabinets, or undertake to send on any mail that arrives, help access personal files on the computer, or even race round to the local pub for a quick last drink together. However, especially if the person has been dismissed, it is quite likely that they won't wish the sad news to be broadcast round the office by a sympathetic colleague. In this case their wishes must be respected. There are those who understandably prefer their departure to be interpreted in other ways – seeking more qualifications, wanting to broaden their horizons, aiming for promotion elsewhere, or simply feeling it was time for a change.

Although it's always upsetting, being made redundant is a common event and it's no disgrace. It will deal a blow to anyone's self-esteem, but younger employees will find it easier to get a new job. Those nearer to retirement age, however, may find it a heavier blow, with far less hope of re-employment, and are therefore more deserving of constructive support and sympathy.

Being Dismissed or Made Redundant

Having just received the dreadful news, your last concern may be how to behave, but there are certain dos and don'ts:

1 Do listen to what is being said to you or read any letter of dismissal carefully.

2 Do try to control your temper and don't say anything you will regret. It is acceptable to display anger, but don't let it descend into abuse.

3 Don't get down on your knees and plead for another chance – it won't make any difference, and dignity, once lost, is hard to recover.

4 Don't seek revenge for dismissal by smashing machines or deleting important files. It will be easy for the authorities to guess who is responsible.

5 Justified complaints against the company who dismissed you are understandable, slander and libel aren't, and won't help your subsequent career.

6 Do try to find time and the mental resources to listen to, and respond to, any kind or helpful things that colleagues are saying.

7 If your departure isn't instant, and a length of notice has to be served, then you should work that notice as professionally as possible.

8 In all the anger and disappointment that may be raging within you, don't overlook your rights and your belongings – you must not leave personal property behind and you mustn't miss out on any severance pay or redundancy money to which you are entitled.

Bad News and How to Handle It

Apart from notices of dismissal, there are other items of bad news that may have to be relayed within an office. Contracts may be lost, perks whittled down, bonuses cancelled, staff facilities reduced – or there may be some bad news of a personal nature, concerning an employee's family. There is always a great temptation to persuade someone else to pass on bad news, but if it is your job, or if it seems right that you do it, then you have to accept that responsibility.

Bad news should be delivered gently, privately and informally. The more serious it is, the more care should be taken in its delivery. If it comes as a shock to the recipient then allowance should be made for any emotional response or bizarre behaviour. Bad news is the time for breaking rules or putting them in abeyance. It is not a time for sticking to protocol.

A Fresh Start

Being forced to leave a job is not necessarily bad news. You may have become stagnant, or trapped in a rut, or you may have bumped up against a glass ceiling, and feel that there is nowhere left for you to go. It is important, therefore, to remain positive about your newly-unemployed status, and see it as an opportunity, rather than the end of the road. As you embark on your new life, set yourself clear targets, for example to find a new job within a certain timeframe. Map out how you are going to achieve this, and start by sitting down and listing all your positive attributes – personality, skills, experience. Looking at this list, think carefully about whether you need to use redundancy as a chance to reset your career – maybe now is the time to make a transition that you've always dreamt of, or to embark on new training. With all this in mind, update your CV so that it reflects all the strengths you have enumerated. Take advice from friends, and make sure that all your contacts know that you are in the job market and looking for a new, and exciting, opportunity.

NOT EVERYTHING THAT IS FACED CAN BE CHANGED. BUT NOTHING CAN BE CHANGED UNTIL IT IS FACED.

James Baldwin

CHAPTER 16

Meetings

One of the greatest sins in the business world is to summon or convene a meeting for which there is no reason. Many people loathe meetings – from the prolonged wait for latecomers and unnecessary formality and pomposity, to the repetitive speeches and the irrelevant subjects that are raised under 'Any Other Business'.

No meeting, therefore, should take place unless there is a good reason for it. It should be well planned, with careful attention paid to the number of people invited to attend, what should and shouldn't be included on the agenda, and the length of time necessary to cover that agenda. If colleagues leave a meeting you have convened feeling that you have wasted their time, then you have done them a disservice. The bigger (or the longer) the meeting, the more you should be sure that you can justify all invitations to it.

Clearly, there is a huge range of meetings – from small informal get-togethers in the department, to video meetings, to large conferences. The rules governing the way meetings are run and how you should behave during them do not vary greatly. All meetings should be efficient. Everyone should come away from any meeting feeling that it has been worthwhile.

Preparation

Every meeting has an organiser, a chairperson, or convenor. If you are calling a meeting and taking responsibility for organising it, then there are a number of matters that you must attend to before that meeting takes place.

Firstly, you have to decide who should attend and every person coming to the meeting must be given reasonable notice. If the meeting is one of a regular series then the date on which it is to take place has probably already been decided and timetabled. If there has been a change in the schedule, then you must make sure the details are circulated in good time; explanatory emails and online calendar invitations are very useful tools when organising get-togethers for large numbers of people. Online calendars will also perform the useful task of reminding attendees about upcoming meetings.

Most meetings that are part of a regular series will include on their agenda minutes of the last meeting. Someone has to prepare these, and this should have been made clear to the person allocated the task before the last meeting, not after it. It is bad business manners to ask anyone to perform a task for which they have had inadequate time to prepare. Minutes of last meetings should be as brief as possible, without omitting anything important.

YOU HAVE A MEETING TO MAKE A DECISION, NOT TO DECIDE ON A QUESTION.

BILL GATES

The Venue

Most meetings are held regularly in the same venue – a boardroom or conference room, or the office of one of the attendees. If, however, you have arranged a meeting in a room that you haven't used earlier for such a purpose, then you should check the room before the meeting takes place.

Any room used for a meeting should be warm, well-ventilated, comfortable. Small group meetings may take place around a desk, or be conducted with people sitting in a circle. The more formal the meeting, however, the better it is to sit everyone attending at a table. This can help establish a focus on the chairperson of the meeting, who should sit either at an end of the table or in the middle position of the side of the table.

If you hope that people will take notes at the meeting, then it's a good idea to supply pads and pencils at each place. This will indicate clearly that you expect those attending to jot down the salient points.

If your meeting requires a white board, perhaps for collaborative thinking or brainstorming, or a screen for PowerPoint presentations, check beforehand that these resources are available, and in the case of the screen, functioning.

If you fear that the meeting is going to be protracted, it is a good idea to supply glasses and a large carafe of water, and perhaps enlist the help of a friendly colleague to bring in coffee and tea at some point in the proceedings.

Agendas

An effective agenda is a secret weapon for all meeting-conveners. It sets out the goals for the meeting, and ensures that attendees' time is not wasted. It should be circulated before the meeting, as it will give team members a chance to prepare themselves (especially if they have been allocated specific reporting tasks).

These are crucial steps in producing a useful agenda:

1. Elicit input from team members/attendees to ensure that all their concerns are addressed. If you find yourself not able to include a suggested item, take the time to explain your reasons to the person who suggested it.

2. Ensure that the topics that are under discussion are relevant to all team members. Too often, meetings get bogged down in discussions that are only really vital to two or three people. You need to ensure that topics under discussion concern the whole meeting, even if it is only on a 'need to know' basis.

3. If your meeting has an overall goal, state it at the top of the agenda as a 'Meeting Objective', eg 'review next quarter's sales goals'.

4. List agenda topics for discussion in as few words as possible, preferably as a question that needs to be answered, eg 'Under what circumstances, if any, should we reallocate office space?', or 'What are the first steps that we should agree in implementing our new social media strategy?'. Questions will direct discussions and drive the meeting towards seeking a resolution.

5. If some of the agenda items are reports of progress, work completed or anticipated, or goals achieved, make this clear: 'Presentation of sales figures for Christmas period' or 'Update on publication programme agreed for Autumn/Winter'.

6. Estimate a realistic amount of time for each topic, including answering questions and group discussion, and add it to the agenda. The time framework should not be used to quash discussion, but simply to give meeting-attendees a realistic expectation.

7 Identify who is responsible for leading each topic – it may well be someone other than the chairperson. This person may have to provide context, explain data, or may be the spokesperson within the organisation for the subject under discussion. They will also appreciate being forewarned.

8 Depending on the nature of your business, it can be a good idea to make the first topic on the agenda, 'review and modify the agenda as needed'. This means that the meeting can briefly ascertain that no late breaking events have intervened to render certain discussions either irrelevant or more pressing.

9 It is conventional to make the last item on the agenda 'Any Other Business', but be aware that this can be an invitation for irrelevant chat and airing of personal preoccupations. If you fear that things will get out of hand, dispense with this item, and simply add 'Summary of Decisions Made', allocating the task of quickly summing up to the chairperson.

DUTIES OF A CHAIRPERSON

Chairing a meeting calls for patience, a sense of humour, diplomacy, an ability to arbitrate, and preparation. Those who are experienced in chairing meetings may have their own methods of ensuring that all goes well. For the rest of us, here are a few points to bear in mind:

- Before inviting anyone to a meeting, make sure that such a meeting is really necessary.
- You should consult others before and after you have drawn up the agenda. Only after you have done that should the agenda be circulated.
- The value or importance of a meeting is not measured by the length of time it takes.
- A good meeting is one where everyone leaves feeling that their point of view has been at least adequately expressed and noted.

I'VE SEARCHED ALL THE PARKS IN ALL THE CITIES – AND FOUND NO STATUES OF COMMITTEES.

G K CHESTERTON

Running a Formal Meeting

Once everyone has been greeted and placed around the table, the chairperson should get the meeting underway at the correct time. Sometimes it's permissible to wait for any important late attendees, apologising to those present for the delay and explaining why this is necessary. In general, however, meetings should start at the appointed time, and adherence to a timetable sets the tone for the rest of the meeting.

It may then be appropriate to introduce those present, or to ask each person to introduce himself or herself. The more formal the meeting, the more the responsibility for introductions lies with the chairperson. If there are outsiders at the meeting, as chairperson you should make sure that everyone is well briefed and that you know the names and roles of each person present. It is bad manners to appear not to know whom you have invited.

Once the meeting is underway, the main duty of a chairperson is to make sure that it proceeds at an efficient rate, that everyone has the opportunity to voice their views, that those who probably have something important to contribute but are shy or hesitant are encouraged to speak, that nobody hijacks the meeting for their own purposes, and that slanging matches are avoided. All this has to be achieved with the right mixture of humour, firmness, impartiality and efficiency.

As chairperson you may put your own views before the meeting, but this is best done after everyone else has done so. You should never appear to predetermine the course and outcome of discussions. Once discussion is underway, you will have to check that it doesn't wander from the point, that people are not simply making the same point over and over again, that everybody is having the opportunity to put their point of view. You must do this without appearing to favour one side over the other.

An easier task is to make sure that the meeting adheres to the agenda. Most people will want to see the meeting moving towards its close as swiftly as possible. However, there is always the risk that your meeting will be attended by someone who likes the sound of their own voice, and enjoys raising 'points of order'. You will need to identify this person and be firmly repressive.

Once the agenda has been discussed, the chairperson should bring the meeting to an end, thanking all present and, if necessary fixing the time and place of the next meeting.

Attending a Formal Meeting

You should prepare for the meeting by reading the minutes of the last meeting and any other relevant notes, and planning what you need to say. If you have been asked to bring figures or materials to a meeting, you should make sure they're ready. If you have been asked to send reports in advance of the meeting to those attending, then you should make sure they are sent in good time. Turning up with the reports of the meeting and expecting everyone to read them there and then is unacceptable.

If you are likely to be late for the meeting, then the usual rules about lateness apply. You should get word to the appropriate person as quickly as possible. It is permissible in such circumstances to ask whoever is chairing the meeting to change the order in which items on the agenda are discussed, but you can't insist on this.

Speaking Up

Once at the meeting, it is simply a matter of deciding when to speak and when to be silent. At formal meetings, all contributions should be channelled through the chairperson, though this procedure may be relaxed as discussions carry on. How well you make your points, how effectively you attract support for your cause, how triumphantly you carry the day will depend on a great many things – personality, preparation, confidence, timing. But it does help to have clear in your mind what your objectives are.

Under no circumstances should you talk over other people, no matter how impassioned you feel. Listen to the person who is speaking, and then interject with a polite 'Bill makes a good point, but I have to say I disagree with his projection…'.

If you feel you are not being given a chance to put forward your point of view, then you may draw the chairperson's attention to this, if the meeting is being conducted on formal lines. Whenever you are taking a line that is against the general feeling of the meeting, it pays to be doggedly persistent, rather than emotionally enraged. If, after a meeting, you do feel that you lost your temper unjustifiably or behaved in some way that was ill-mannered, then you should send a letter of apology to the chairperson as soon as possible. You should not apologise for your views, but only the way you expressed them.

WHEN THE OUTCOME OF A MEETING IS TO HAVE ANOTHER MEETING, IT HAS BEEN A LOUSY MEETING.

HERBERT HOOVER

Minutes of Meetings

The record that is kept of meeting, the minutes, performs the following useful functions:

- Minutes are a record of a group's decisions and actions.
- They are a reminder of who was assigned specific tasks, and what they are.
- They are evidence of deadlines.
- They are beneficial for people who were absent when decisions were made.

Formal Minutes

These are used to document official decisions, and are commonly circulated by charities, government departments, public companies, schools:

Formal Meeting Minutes [Example]
Company + Department Name

Date

1. Call to Order
[Chair] called to order the regular meeting of [Organisation] on [date] at [location]

2. Roll Call
[Secretary] conducted a roll call. The following persons were present
[List of attendees]

3. Approval of minutes from last meeting
[Secretary] read the minutes of the last meeting. The minutes were approved.

4. Open issues
Open issue + Summary of discussion
Open issue + Summary of discussion

5. New business
New business + Summary of discussion
New business + Summary of discussion

6. Adjournment
7. [Chair] adjourned the meeting at [time meeting ended]

Minutes submitted by: [Name]

Minutes approved by: [Name]

Informal Minutes

Informal minutes are a concise record of important topics that have been covered in your meeting such as goals, deadlines, new ideas, and they serve to document key points and actions.

These are the key elements you should include in your minutes (lay the page out as spaciously and clearly as possible):

1. Date and time of the meeting.
2. Names of the participants and any people who weren't able to attend.
3. Purpose of the meeting. This should explain why the meeting was called and what it was trying to achieve. This can be quite specific: 'Meeting to Discuss Planned New Product Lines for Summer Season', or more general 'Weekly Team Meeting'.
4. Agenda items and topics discussed. Here, the minutes should follow the headings of the meeting agenda, and the minutes-taker should record key discussion points and decisions.
5. Action items. If the meeting has been productive, actions will be assigned to key participants. Record any decisions or action items, and then add them to the specific agenda topics. If actions emerge from the meeting that are not germane to the topics originally outlined in the agenda, you can add an Actions category at the end of the minutes.
6. Next meeting date and place, and if possible some guidance about the topic of discussion.

Try and circulate meeting notes as soon as possible after the meeting, as they will act as an *aide-mémoire* for participants who have been allocated specific tasks.

Video Meetings

Increasingly, people are utilising modern technology to conduct meetings online, using programs such as Zoom, Microsoft Teams, or Google Meet.

While the meeting may follow the parameters that have been outlined for conventional meetings, the technology does present particular issues. Video meetings will run much more smoothly if they are efficiently moderated. The moderator should ensure that the agenda is adhered to, but they are also responsible for a number of video-related issues.

If you are the moderator you should use the waiting room function to control the pace at which people enter the meeting. This will allow you time to greet every joining participant by name and, if necessary, make introductions.

Monitor all the meeting participants and be aware when people are trying to speak – it helps if people raise their hands. Video meetings can easily deteriorate into a cacophony of people talking over each other, and they will run much more smoothly if each speaker pauses after delivery, giving the moderator the chance to pass the baton to a new participant.

When the meeting ends, announce that you are going to summarise the salient points – this will indicate to the other participants that they must give you the floor, and not interrupt.

Preparing for a Video Call

Look at your preview image on screen and make sure that your background is bland and doesn't convey the wrong image. A neat bookshelf might be acceptable, but any signs of disorder – unruly piles of paper or books, discarded clothes – will ring alarm bells. If all else fails, you can always choose a standard screen background (though people will inevitably wonder about the multitude of sins it's concealing). Natural light from a window that diffuses the room evenly is the best and most flattering option. You can also place a light in front of you and behind your computer, which will help to focus on your face. Never place a light behind you – you'll look like a silhouette and fellow meeting-participants will be squinting into a bright light.

Take the time to brush your hair, find a reasonably smart shirt. Sit up straight and don't slouch and you will project a more efficient image.

VIDEO MISTAKES

Remember that everyone can see your face clearly on-screen, all the time. Video calls give you unrelenting exposure, so don't allow yourself to forget that you're on display. On the other hand, don't stare at your own face on-screen when you should be listening attentively to other people.

1. Arrive at the meeting in good time – allow a little extra time for technical glitches and computers running slow.
2. Don't fiddle with your face, or beard, or hair when other people are talking.
3. Don't multitask; it's quite obvious when you're looking at other windows on your computer or fiddling with your phone.
4. Turn off your phone to stop notifications, or at least mute it.
5. It is acceptable to sip a tea or coffee or glass of water, but don't slurp and never eat on-screen.
6. Try and sit still and don't go over the top with your hand gestures – excess movement can cause video to freeze and you may find yourself stuck in a comical pose.
7. If you're using your laptop, put it on a firm surface and leave it there. Any movement of the laptop will be exaggerated, and walking around with it will make everyone feel seasick.
8. Not turning on your camera is a bad idea in a business context, as it advertises the fact that you are not engaged with the topic and people will start to speculate about what you're actually doing. In certain instances you can explicitly ask permission to 'monitor' the meeting with half an ear.
9. Beware grandstanding. Unless you're actually presenting, it's a good idea to pause regularly to give other participants a chance to jump in.
10. When you're not actually speaking, use non-verbal reactions – smiling, nodding etc – to indicate that you are listening to what is being said, and are engaged with the topic.

Chapter 17
Public Speaking & Presentations

We have myriad ways of communicating in the 21st century, but there is nothing so persuasive as face-to-face interaction. Unlike communication in writing, or even through a camera lens, it is possible to build trust very quickly. It is equally easy to lose it.

Whether you are making a speech to a large audience at a conference hall, or presenting to a small gathering of colleagues in the office meeting room, the basic principles are the same.

Making speeches or delivering effective presentations is all about certain techniques that can be learnt and utilised to your advantage. Most importantly of all, careful presentation will help to mitigate nerves, enabling you to show yourself at your best.

What Makes a Great Speaker?

A great speaker should have a strong message, conveyed with personality. The ancient Greeks were the first people to recognise this. Aristotle argued that there is a trinity of rhetorical values:

- Logos: an appeal to rational arguments
- Pathos: a call on emotions
- Ethos: character/personality

Whilst these three are intrinsically linked, logos and pathos are associated with message or content, and ethos with delivery. It is delivery that presents most people with the greatest challenge.

THERE ARE ALWAYS THREE SPEECHES, FOR EVERY ONE YOU ACTUALLY GAVE. THE ONE YOU PRACTICED, THE ONE YOU GAVE, AND THE ONE YOU WISH YOU GAVE.

DALE CARNEGIE

Why Don't Most Speeches Work?

Most speeches fall flat because they lack one of the above ingredients, and more often than not, it is personality that is missing. It is a commonly held misconception that some people are just born with the ability to hold an audience or to entertain; some people describe this as 'the gift of the gab'. In truth, it is entirely possible to become a great speaker through the application of some simple techniques and a bit of practice. It is important to understand that you will be at your most effective when you are relaxed and when you feel you have the attention of the audience.

Typically, you would then speak in the same way as you would at a relaxed social occasion, including conversational language and plenty of pauses, during which eye contact is made with the audience. These are all too often the very elements that are missing in formal speeches. How often are speakers racked with nerves and find themselves rushing through their speech? How often does shyness and a desire not to lose their place on a script prevent meaningful eye contact?

Speakers often believe that a formal occasion requires clever language and long words – the very things that obscure understanding and prevent a connection between speaker and audience. The most compelling speakers have a style that is closer to normal conversation than you might imagine.

Overcoming Fear

A speaker who cannot convey confidence will undermine their message. The audience cannot tell the difference between a speaker who lacks self-confidence and one who lacks confidence in the message they are giving.

It is possible to be over-confident as well as under-confident. An audience is just as likely to warm to someone who is a little nervous as they are to dislike someone who comes across as over-confident or cocky.

For most people, conquering nerves is just a question of focusing on the presentation (and not the nerves), preparing well (including rehearsing), and adopting a positive mindset. Once they get over the first few minutes, nerves subside to a more manageable level. Most find that the more they present, the less nervous they become.

A few simple things will help to create the impression of confidence:

Smiling

Firstly, smile (however hard this might be) and ensure that you relax your body, in spite of the fact that this requires considerable effort. If you manage to look relaxed, the audience will reflect their belief in your confidence back to you, and your confidence will grow. If you can smile at your audience, you will fool your brain that you are happy and confident, and that in turn becomes genuine happiness and confidence. This makes you more relaxed and it becomes easier to smile.

Some people's fear of public speaking is deeply embedded. They may find that nerves can peak during the middle of a presentation, a feeling that does not evaporate until long after the presentation is finished. In fact, they can experience anxiety just by thinking about presentations. If this is the case for you, the issue may need a little more attention. Many people find that it is worth investing in hypnotherapy or counselling.

Eye Contact

Eye contact underscores the importance of your words and sends a subliminal signal to the listener to think about what has been said.

Not making eye contact sends a different subliminal signal. It either tells the listener not to pay attention to what you have said because you don't believe it yourself, or it implies that your statement was not very important. When people talk about not trusting someone, they often use phrases such as 'they couldn't look me in the eye'. This is as much the case for speaking to a large audience as it is for one-on-one conversations.

It is important to minimise the amount of time spent looking at notes when not speaking, but it is perfectly acceptable to glance at them while you are. In fact, sometimes it is a really good idea to do so – such as when you're quoting someone. Reading short quotes or critical details directly from the page will serve to emphasise the importance of the words and the fact that you are working hard to do justice to them.

Having established the importance of eye contact, many people worry that the need for notes or even a full script prevents them from making good eye contact. This challenge is easily overcome. All you need to do is make sure that your script or notes are well laid out, and make judicious use of pauses.

Pausing and Silence

If there is one thing that will transform a speaker's ability, it is a willingness to embrace silence. Whether in a podium speech or in a one-on-one conversation, it is pausing that allows comprehension and conveys conviction.

The other important thing about pausing is that it simply reflects what we do in natural conversation. The very best speakers don't speak at us; they make us feel as if we are in a conversation with them. Pausing is the single most useful tool to help us achieve this.

There are two types of pause:

PAUSING BEFORE SPEAKING

- Draws the audience's attention, creating a sense of anticipation
- Allows the speaker to take ownership of the occasion
- Allows the speaker to draw breath
- Allows the speaker to think – and not use disfluencies (ums and ers)
- Provides an opportunity for eye contact (and smiling)

PAUSING AFTER SPEAKING

- Allows the audience to think about what has been said
- Asks permission from the audience to go on

It can be challenging to introduce deliberate pauses into your speech, as we are all aware that humans are uncomfortable with silence. Public speakers fear silence because they are worried that the audience will think they have forgotten what they were going to say, or will interrupt.

When you are in the spotlight you can easily lose your sense of time, and a split-second of silence can feel like a lifetime.

You must learn to live with silence, as if there is one thing that will transform the abilities of a speaker, it is the ability to pause.

Preparing your Notes

The way in which notes for a speech are laid out on the page can have a transformative impact on how it is delivered. If notes are written in the same way as an essay, in a linear fashion, using complete sentences and a small typeface, you will deliver them as if you are reading an essay.

The first step is to use a large font, which will be easy to read. Next, think about which words are really needed and take out all extraneous ones to make the language sound conversational. You can also take out the connecting words such as and, if, but and also.

Having fewer words on the page makes the notes easier to follow. Additionally, the fact that the speaker has to think a little about the text, rather than just reading it off the page, creates a more natural performance.

Writing your Speech or Presentation

Every speech or presentation should have a purpose, and it is this purpose that should be foremost in the writer's mind. The main purposes are:

1. To entertain (such as an after-dinner speech)
2. To inspire
3. To persuade
4. To inform

Of course, if all you had to do was inform people, you could just send an email and not waste people's time getting them together and talking to them. A public speaking opportunity should be primarily about inspiring and persuading. If being entertaining is helpful to your cause and you are comfortable with it, you can do that too.

> I'VE LEARNED THAT PEOPLE WILL FORGET WHAT YOU SAID, PEOPLE WILL FORGET WHAT YOU DID, BUT PEOPLE WILL NEVER FORGET HOW YOU MADE THEM FEEL.
> Maya Angelou

Expectations

Any speech or presentation not written with the audience and the occasion in mind is at risk of missing the target. You can mitigate this risk by asking the questions set out below. You may be able to answer these for yourself, but if you are speaking at an external event you will need to speak to the organiser for more details.

- What is the audience expecting?
- What does the audience know about the subject?
- Is this new information? (has anyone else spoken about this subject to them?)
- What do they want to know?
- Are they interested in the subject?
- Is it contentious?

In addition, you should find out about the arrangements for your speech. Who is speaking before and after you? Where do you appear in the programme? Are you first or last? Are you running up to a hard stop (lunch or end of day)? Is there audiovisual equipment you can use? Can you plug your product or business?

Finding Your Theme

The secret to writing a good speech or presentation is to know what its central or main point is. The theme should not be too abstract. For example, a presentation that has a theme entitled the 'The future of our business' is vague and open-ended, and gives little direction to the person writing it – or, indeed, to the audience. A presentation entitled 'The future of our business outside the EU' might provide a little more direction. But the idea could be developed further to make it sound more urgent, engaging and optimistic – for example: 'The important opportunities that await us outside of the EU, and what we must do now'.

STRUCTURE

Good presenters, who know their subject inside out, understand how to reveal enough information to create both a level of understanding and an appetite for more.

The structure of your speech or presentation should be dictated by your purpose. Think in terms of the messages that you would like people to remember. Having three main messages is probably about right to support your theme. Ensure that you explain each one in a way that is clear, engaging and memorable. You can use any of the following to help you convey your message, but don't use too many of these techniques and never forget the point you are trying to make:

- Provide examples.
- Use metaphors or similes.
- Use illustrations.
- Use anecdotal evidence.
- Use storytelling structures.
- Use humour.
- Provide pictures.
- Use quotes.
- Provide empirical evidence (facts, figures, charts, references).
- Include endorsements of other people who share your views.

> ACCORDING TO MOST STUDIES, PEOPLE'S NUMBER ONE FEAR IS PUBLIC SPEAKING. NUMBER TWO IS DEATH. DEATH IS NUMBER TWO. DOES THAT SOUND RIGHT? THIS MEANS TO THE AVERAGE PERSON, IF YOU GO TO A FUNERAL, YOU'RE BETTER OFF IN THE CASKET THAN DOING THE EULOGY.
>
> JERRY SEINFELD

DURATION

Our attention spans are all finite and, however fascinating a presentation is, we will find ourselves becoming restless after a while because we want to interact with the speaker (for example by challenging their view, endorsing it, or just asking questions).

Anecdotal evidence suggests that 20 minutes is 'about right'. However, more often than not, the time period a speaker has to fill is beyond their control; you may be given a slot of 40 minutes, or more. You can break up longer speaking slots by doing the following:

- Take a break – give people a chance to chat, check their phones and then re-focus.

- Show a video.

- Show images (accompanied by recorded commentary or music).

- Present the audience with a question and ask them to spend a few minutes discussing it before giving you an answer.

- Conduct a poll on an issue related to your topic (ask for a show of hands or use an electronic system).

Perhaps more important than the overall length of the presentation is finishing it in time to ensure there is an opportunity for people to ask questions. If you have a Q&A session at the end you will find out exactly what your audience wants to know and be able to provide them with the information they need.

Delivering a Presentation

The start of the presentation offers a unique opportunity. It is this moment when the speaker most commands the audience's attention and it should not be squandered.

Stammering out an introduction, thanking the audience for the invitation to speak, outlining the upcoming speech in excruciating detail, apologising for lateness (or for the fact that the speech might be cut short because of time constraints), are all bad starts.

It is always best to get someone else to introduce you where possible. That way, your first words can have real impact. You will not find yourself sidetracked by self-introductions or explanations about who you are, which may make you sound like you're pleading for acceptance or validation.

The start of your speech needs to present you as someone with confidence, competence and a message worth listening to. Start by saying something that will at least capture the audience's attention for that moment – it could include a few hooks to spike their curiosity. The following can serve as strong starts:

- Challenging the perceived wisdom (for example with a single quote).

- Asking a rhetorical question.

- A joke (if it is funny and you can carry it off).

- A story (if it holds attention, has a point and gets to it quickly).

- An inducement – or in other words 'if you pay attention to this presentation, you will be wiser, richer or ahead of the pack'.

IT USUALLY TAKES ME MORE THAN THREE WEEKS TO PREPARE A GOOD IMPROMPTU SPEECH.

Mark Twain

Language

The best language to use in any form of public speaking is simple language. When speakers use elaborate language, we consciously or subconsciously conclude that they are trying to hide something.

Many people make the mistake of preparing for a presentation by sitting down at their laptop. The language that emerges is written language which, when spoken, sounds awkward and stilted. It is much better to start with a series of 'headlines', and to sketch out the development of your ideas in note form, dispensing with linking phrases and prepositions, so you will be forced to extemporise and ad lib.

Speakers feel that they are honouring their audience or the occasion by using formal language. Given that very few us are called to speak at the United Nations Assembly, or to address members of the House of Commons or Lords, there is little need for elevated language. Besides, we know that simple language is best however auspicious the occasion.

This speech by Winston Churchill vividly illustrates how simple language can have a rhetorical impact:
'We shall go on to the end, we shall fight in France,
we shall fight on the seas and oceans,
we shall fight with growing confidence and growing strength in the air, we shall defend our Island, whatever the cost may be.'

Follow this example, and use short words and short sentences. Resist using caveats and qualifications – just project absolute certainty.

If you have an important point to make, don't try to be subtle or clever. Use a pile driver. Hit the point once. Then come back and hit it again. Then hit it a third time – a tremendous whack.
Winston Churchill

Persuading and Presenting

The term 'presentation' is an unhelpful one. To present is to put something in front of someone and then walk away. What speakers should do is persuade and move people either emotionally or from one perspective to another. If all they have to do is to present information, they should simply write an email and press send.

Think of almost every presentation as an opportunity to persuade people. This requires you to do more than just put facts in front of people and hope that they come to the right conclusion for themselves.

- You must convince your audience of a need or cause, or that you believe in a particular product or programme.

- You must convince your audience to share your conviction.

- You must convince your audience that their involvement will be beneficial.

You will able to achieve these goals by demonstrating to your listeners that you have researched them and understand their values, which you will then reflect in your presentation.

If you need the audience to change behaviours, make it clear that 'other people are already doing this'. Let the audience know who else has subscribed to your view and provide examples where people are already doing what you propose.

Take time to establish your authority and reputation. Explain to the audience how much knowledge and experience you have in the subject. Let them know your qualifications, achievements and endorsements. You may need to do this subtly for some audiences.

Preparing and Using Visuals

Many people start writing a presentation by preparing their visuals (photographs, charts, slides), in the belief that these aids are the most effective way of conveying the message. In fact, a competent speaker who has taken time to structure an interesting and articulate message is much more persuasive than the most elaborate slide deck.

Some people also believe that in addition to being the core of the presentation, the slides can act as speaking notes and handouts. This is not true – in fact, all the slides should do is support the themes and the messages of the presenter. If there is a need for handouts, visuals and speaking notes, these should be prepared separately.

In the world of business, particularly, there is a belief that a presentation without visuals is not really a presentation at all. Nothing could be further from the truth.

How to Close a Presentation

There is an old adage that to close a presentation you should just 'tell 'em what you told 'em', ie repeat the contents of your presentation in summary form. In fact, this is boring and predictable and adds nothing of any significance to your presentation.

Your closing should certainly act as a summary, but in a way that is memorable and inspiring. If you need people to take action, conclude with a 'call to action', or at least reiterate the consequences of not taking action. Ensure that people go away knowing what to do, what message to spread, or how to involve themselves further in your cause.

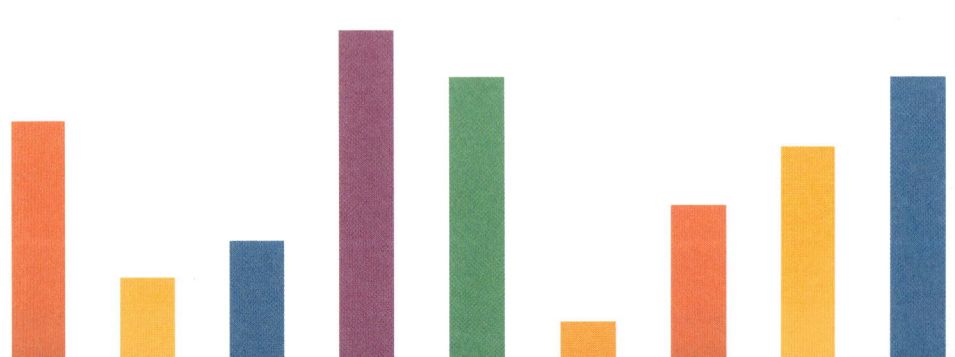

THE MOST PRECIOUS THINGS IN A SPEECH ARE THE PAUSES.

Sir Ralph Richardson

Question and Answer Sessions

Many people put a great deal of effort into planning out their speech or presentation, but often forget to prepare for questions.

Just one question from an audience member can undo all of the good work from the presentation. However, if that one question is given a good answer, this can start to win over even the most sceptical audience.

Preparations for Questions

If you are having a Q&A session at the end of your presentation, it is important to prepare for it, particularly if your role is to persuade people. If you don't give people a chance to explore your thinking or to challenge you on detail, they will feel that you are hiding something.

It is not enough simply to prepare your presentation and leave time at the end to field a few questions. You must actively prepare for the closing interrogation by trying to anticipate what questions will be asked (as well as planning for the ones you really don't want to hear). Consult with friends and colleagues, so you can assemble a long list of potential questions.

Prepare answers for all the questions, and practise delivering them. Review your answers and decide if you need to change the presentation. It may be that some of the ideas and information you have uncovered during the process are better placed as part of the main presentation. For example, if an issue is contentious, not mentioning it might draw attention to the fact that it is something you would rather avoid. Addressing a subject head-on shows that you are not worried by it, and you won't be wrong-footed by a spontaneous, and challenging, question.

How to Structure an Answer

The principles for structuring an answer are the same as for structuring a presentation: it must have a point, and all other aspects of the answer must support the point. Once a question has been asked, address it directly. Do not talk around the subject; to demur would suggest dishonesty or evasion. If you cannot provide a direct answer because the subject is complex or sensitive, say so before answering the question as best you can.

Top Tips for Answering Questions

- Tackle every question as if it is another opportunity to sell your idea (ie in a positive and engaging way).

- If you don't know the answer it is best to say so rather than trying to bluff. If you say, 'I don't know' you will have been honest and will get some credit.

- If things are becoming really difficult, have some helpful phrases to hand such as 'what I can say is this…'. This will make it look like you are trying to help and that you are on the side of the questioner.

- Be quick – most questions should be answered in less than a minute. That way you get to answer more questions and the audience don't feel like you are stalling.

- If the question has a negative aspect to it, don't avoid the negativity. Instead, look to conclude your answer on a positive note.

- If there are untruths in the question, it is essential that you address them head-on before answering the question.

Fielding Difficult Questions

Q&As are not a competition between questioner and speaker. Approach every question as if it has been asked in good faith (they usually are). Be calm and patient with the questioner. Clarify the question if necessary. People don't always have enough information to be clear.

Don't repeat the question unless the audience may not have heard it. Repeating the question can look like you are stalling for time or are patronising the questioner.

Don't begin your response with the words 'good question'. You may look like you planted the question or that you hoped you would not be asked it and are over-compensating. It is also insulting to other questioners whom you did not compliment.

Finally, don't let Q&A sessions drag on too long, or the audience will get perceptibly restless. If you audience is struck dumb and nobody ventures to ask a question, give it a few moments, then finish with a friendly sign-off such as 'Well, I guess I must have covered all the points! Thank you for listening.'

Soft Skills

CHAPTER 18

Walking into a room full of strangers or being introduced to new people can be daunting for many of us, and within a business environment we may find ourselves repeatedly facing this challenge. There is a sense that everyone is looking at us and that they are judging us – we feel uncomfortable and under pressure.

And yet, some people can enter a room and turn every head. They exude grace and charm; they instil confidence in everyone around them. So what are they doing that the rest of us are not?

To flourish in the world of work we need to understand why meeting people presents such a challenge and learn why these first few seconds are so vital. There are simple strategies that will not only make the whole process easier, but will also make you look and feel more confident.

First Impressions

Ask how long it takes to make a first impression, and you will get a pretty consistent answer of 'around a handful of seconds'. The reality is that it is not possible to give a scientifically precise answer. People will typically say that they 'don't like to make snap decisions', that they like to give people the 'benefit of the doubt' or even that it is rude to make quick judgments. This is all worthy, but largely untrue. We all are quick to judge.

Think of all the people you meet in a working day. Some will be fleeting exchanges; others will be with people you end up doing business with for years. If you assume the best in others, and resist the impulse to make an instant judgment, you allow a greater possibility of forming positive relationships with more people.

Getting Better at Making a Great First Impression

One of the best ways of getting better at something is to watch people who are already good at it and copy what they do. The secret is to break down each element of what a person does successfully into constituent elements and think of these as separate activities. Then look at why doing things in a particular way might be helpful. Finally, you put all of the elements back together. This is known as 'modelling'.

There will be plenty of people in your everyday life who make a great first impression, and we can also look for inspiration to people who have to do this as a critical part of their day job. Celebrities, politicians and actors are often good at it. They do it a lot and they also do it in front of the camera. This gives us a chance to study what they do in some detail.

Constituents of Great First Impressions

1. Smiling
2. Eye contact
3. Body language
4. Pacing

If making a great first impression only consists of doing four things, why do some of us find it so hard? Put very simply, it is because we are human, which is to say the first impressions we give are continually being sabotaged by our animal instincts.

Because survival relied on getting judgments about friends and foes (and their intentions) right all of the time, the part of the brain that deals with threats and fear (the amygdala) is well developed. In addition we have a non-conscious negativity bias, a basic survival skill, which means we seek out and pay more attention to body language and signals that could be suspicious. It is therefore not surprising that we are naturally suspicious of new people and new situations.

In high-pressure situations – such as the start of a job interview or even just walking alone into a networking event – your brain will try to help you by defaulting to instinctive behaviour. As your instinctive brain naturally defaults to caution, you are likely to be at the mercy of whatever biases and prejudices you carry around with you.

It takes a conscious decision to switch off the internal signals that tell you to be cautious, but it's a decision you have the power to make, and if you do it consistently, you will steadily become less suspicious or circumspect.

It is important to remember that the more confident you look, the more trustworthy you appear to other people. They will then reflect that trust back to us. This creates a positive cycle as opposed to a negative one.

Smiling

It has been said that you are never fully dressed without a smile, and it is the most important element of a first impression. Why is a smile so important? It is the first expression we experiment with as a baby, and a smile is recognised around the globe (albeit there are some nuances in different cultures). As the well-worn cliché goes, when you smile, the world really does smile with you.

A smile says a number of things:

- I'm confident.
- I'm pleased to be here.
- I believe in myself and what I'm saying.
- Perhaps most importantly, without use of words, it allows us to say 'I am pleased to meet you'.

Smiling will ensure that you make that vital connection when you first enter a room. If you smile at others, there is a good chance that they will smile back. You will already be aware that you smile when you are happy and when you feel positive about the people around you. In other words, the smile is not just for the benefit of those who see it – there is a cause and effect on the body, ie I smile when I am happy, and when I smile, I become happy.

Real or Fake?

There are, of course, two sorts of smile, real and fake. But what is the difference?

It is all in the eyes. A real or full smile associated with positive emotions is more likely to create eye creases and a fake smile will not. While identifying a fake smile is not inevitably straightforward or accurate, it seems reasonable to assume that, if you can reframe the conditions just a little, less faking is required. For example, if you feel under pressure at an interview, you can smile when you meet the interviewer because you are genuinely grateful for the fact that you have made it to the interview, rather than because you are consciously thinking 'now is when I must smile'.

But even if you have to fake a smile, you still get the benefit – and so do the people you smile at.

Listen to that Smile

There are many ways in which you can confer joy and happiness when you meet people, and a smile is the most obvious. But what if you can't see people? Does that mean you just have to fall back on friendly words? In fact, you must keep smiling because the people you speak to can hear a smile. A smile changes the shape of the lips and the soft tissue of the palate, and we hear it as clearly as we can see micro (or macro) expressions in the face. In fact, if in a phone call you use emollient words but don't smile, you will start ringing alarm bells in people's brains. They will hear in your voice that you don't mean it.

WEAR A SMILE AND HAVE FRIENDS; WEAR A SCOWL AND HAVE WRINKLES.

GEORGE ELIOT

Overcoming Shyness

Making eye contact presents a great challenge for many of us because we are shy. For shy people, the act of connecting through strong eye contact feels intrusive or perhaps challenging. This highlights the very simple but important point that what is enough eye contact for some people is too much for others. Studies have shown that when we look at a face, we are reading its micro signals, and this uses up a great deal of mental capacity.

Eye Contact

Which of us wasn't told by our parents to make sure we look people in the eye when we talked to them? Why is eye contact so important? Most people would say that it is has something to do with building trust, and that it is somehow related to showing confidence. They would also be likely to agree that eye contact is universally recognised – in other words, eye contact is much like smiling, in that it means the same thing to everyone around the world. Whilst this is true, it is only true up to a point. There are important nuances and differences in how eye contact is perceived in the various regions of the world.

The problem with eye contact is that it's the first thing that we fail to do when we are feeling nervous and unconfident, and if our eye contact falters, we look shifty – it's a telltale sign that we are trying to deceive, and thus we really do have a reason not to be trusted.

When we meet people, we are looking for the signs that help us determine whether or not to trust them. It is therefore safer for our subconscious mind to assume that we can't trust that person if they don't look us in the eye – or if we can't see their eyes.

How Much Eye Contact?

Research indicates that three seconds of eye contact is average, and that no one is comfortable with eye contact that goes on for longer than nine seconds. It is critical to remember that you should try and work out what is comfortable for the other person rather than think about what is right for you. An intense gimlet-eyed stare will inevitably disconcert rather than reassure.

There are plenty of reasons that prevent us from making eye contact. Some, such as sunglasses, can be easily sorted. Even if you are meeting someone in the hottest, brightest weather, take off your sunglasses briefly. This does two things – not only does it allow that all-important eye contact at the critical moment of meeting, but it shows that you are making a special effort for the person you have just met.

Perhaps a more common barrier to making eye contact in this day and age is the ubiquitous mobile phone screen. You cannot effectively listen to people, and they won't feel that they are really speaking to you, if you only have eyes for your device. Whilst it is technically possible to talk or listen whilst looking at your phone, you invariably end up doing at least one of these two tasks ineffectively. Talking and listening to the people in front of you is important, so put screens away.

Don't let talking to a group of people deter you from maintaining eye contact. Choose one person you can focus upon and imagine that you are addressing your remarks to that person only. Look at the person you have chosen until you have finished your sentence. Then move on, and choose another person to address. This technique will stop your eyes swivelling around in a desperate attempt to include the whole group, which can look shifty and therefore disconcerting.

> BODY LANGUAGE IS A VERY POWERFUL TOOL. WE HAD BODY LANGUAGE BEFORE WE HAD SPEECH, AND APPARENTLY, EIGHTY PER CENT OF WHAT YOU UNDERSTAND IN A CONVERSATION IS READ THROUGH THE BODY, NOT THE WORDS.
> DEBORAH BULL, BALLERINA

Body Language

The process that drives the signals we send is, at its most simple, 'fight or flight', or at least the preparation for it, which triggers certain responses. The fact that the body is undertaking these internal processes is betrayed by outward physical behaviours (or signals), eg a smile or a frown, and both you and the people around you react to these phenomena.

How do you send out the positive signals that show you are confident? The easy answer is to be confident and then the physical behaviours you project will reflect this. But if you aren't confident, what can you do? The answer is you must change your body language to feel and look more confident.

What are Your Tells?

The great professional card players have all manner of techniques up their sleeves to give them an edge or an advantage. One such advantage is the ability to read people. They will watch their opponents as they turn over their cards and look for signs that might indicate what hand they have been dealt. They will also look to see how this changes as the game unfolds. The signs that players look out for are known as 'tells', and they betray critical emotions such as delight (at a brilliant hand), disappointment (at a bad one), confidence or nervousness.

Some people describe the phenomenon of inadvertently indicating our inner emotions through physical signals as 'emotional leakage'. In other words, our real emotions are leaking out of our bodies whether we know it or not, and often in spite of our best efforts to prevent it.

Fie, fie upon her! There's language in her eye, her cheek, her lip, Nay, her foot speaks; her wanton spirits look out at every joint and motive of her body.
William Shakespeare

If you want to detect these signs, first look at the hands and feet:

- A clenched fist
- Hands locked together
- A hand buried firmly in a pocket (possibly with a clenched fist)
- Gripping an object (such as a pen or lectern)
- Repeatedly clicking a pen
- A tapping foot

And then look to the face and the rest of the body:

- Shifting stiffly from one foot to the other
- A stiff and unmoving face or frown
- A tight throat (often indicated by a higher pitched and/or less modulated voice)
- Shallow breathing
- Stiff arms and wrists

One of the big contrasts between people who project confidence and those who don't is summed up by the idea of open and closed body language. People whose body language is closed tend to look like they are trying to make themselves smaller. Their head is down, shoulders are hunched, and their arms are held close to their body. Those with open body language are the polar opposite. They hold their shoulders back and their head is held up (better for smiling and making eye contact). They stand tall and gesture freely, and there is a relaxed looseness to them. People with open body language subliminally tell anyone watching that they have nothing to hide.

How to Improve Your Body Language

The answer is simple: learn to recognise what you do when you are nervous and stop doing it. You can identify what betrays your nervousness by self-appraisal and by seeking help from friends and colleagues in pinning down your tells. Don't give the game away by telling them what you think you do – just ask them and see what they come up with.

Ideally, you will enlist friends and colleagues to observe you when you are under pressure – for example, when you are talking to people who make you uncomfortable, such as your boss. If possible, they might observe you giving a presentation and be able to identify the way your behaviour changes. The chances are that your nervousness will be reflected though tension in your body and through trying to make yourself smaller. The mnemonic TIGER is a simple and practical way of addressing both of these problems:

T Tauten your abdominal muscles. This will give your voice that lovely centred resonance.

I Inhale: breathe slowly and properly, with your stomach out as you inhale. Be careful that you don't breathe into your shoulders as you won't inhale as much oxygen.

G Grow: stand tall but with your feet firmly on the ground. Stretch yourself to your full height by imagining that you are being pulled upwards with an invisible piece of string. At the same time roll your shoulders back. (This process also works when sitting down).

E Equalise: distribute your weight equally on each foot – to do otherwise means tensing up one of your legs, making you look unsteady. Relaxing and feeling the ground beneath your feet makes you feel … grounded!

R Relax: relax your extremities – your hands and arms for example – so your gestures look natural. If you can, relax your face and neck so that your voice and words don't sound too strained.

THE HUMAN BODY IS THE BEST PICTURE OF THE HUMAN SOUL.

Ludwig Wittgenstein

Pacing

If you ask people to name the things that make their colleagues stand out as confident, most will suggest smiling, eye contact and body language. Whilst these are correct, there is a fourth component that few people will consciously notice but of which they will subconsciously be aware. It is arguably the most important, and is in fact the one that most of us should think a little bit more about. It is pacing.

The observation that 'a gentleman or woman is never in a hurry' reflects the fact that being calm and unhurried makes you look in control, confident and elegant. You only have to think about Hollywood stars on the red carpet – part of their act is to remain unhurried in front of the cameras. They need to ensure that they are not sending out a message that says, 'I would rather be somewhere else'.

Take your Time

We rush when we are under pressure because our body is on high alert, probably because we are suffering from social anxiety. Whenever we experience panic, our bodies initiate the built-in threat responses in preparation to fight or to run.

This can cause us to tense up, smile less and make less eye contact. The adrenaline rush we experience confuses our perception of time; we perceive time to be running much faster than it actually is, and our actions speed up to match. We find we walk much more quickly, talk much more quickly, and what might have passed for comfortable pauses in conversation now seem like eternal embarrassing silences that we feel we must fill.

Unfortunately, this behaviour is highly contagious: other people pick up on, and experience, our anxiety. We often find that when people meet socially, especially for the first time, they are 'high energy', in that they talk quickly and loudly and move rapidly.

How to Get it Right

Think about an occasion when you have to walk into a room and meet new people. It could be a networking event or even an interview:

- Slow down and breathe. Before you enter a room, take a deep breath in through your nose to the count of four and then breathe out through your mouth to the same count. In, two, three, four, out, two, three, four.

- Ideally repeat this three times.

- Walk into the room.

- Be your brilliant best.

By doing this you are resetting your body, switching off your fight or flight alerts. It will instantly make you feel and appear calmer, and you will actually be much more in control.

A lot of people think they have to be 'high energy' to make a strong impression, and fear that if they are not energetic they will be seen as unenthusiastic or disinterested. But when this conscious attempt to be lively meets natural anxiety it can give off the wrong message, so slow it down.

When you slow down and calm down, you will find you have the time and space to truly and actively listen to what the other person has to say. You will be less likely to interrupt them and they will be flattered at how interested you appear in them. Slowing things down is a great way of showing respect.

Many people believe that the secret to being charismatic, or to having a strong presence, is to be present in the moment. The secret is to think less about yourself and more about the other person.

1, 2, 3, 4 …

Communication Styles

CHAPTER 19

The Difference in Communication Between Men and Women

Inevitably, there is as much variation within gender as there is between genders. Context is key – different contexts generate different styles of speech. However, in mixed groups, men tend to dominate the exchange. Research has shown that women don't get equal airtime until they dominate the group numerically.

Direct or Indirect Speech?

Whether your speech is direct or indirect depends on how much or how little context is used when communicating.

Direct communication uses very little context, whereas indirect uses a great deal. The variations are very noticeable between cultures and countries. In the West, there is generally a perception that direct speech is rude and dominating and indirect is polite and collaborative.

LANGUAGE LADDER: DIRECT TO INDIRECT

- Report?
- Give me the report.
- Hand me the report from last year please.
- Could you pass me the report from last year please?
- Would you be so kind as to pass me the report with all of last year's results please?
- You know that report with all of last year's financial performance statistics? Would it be possible to let me take a look when you have a moment? Thank you.

Arguably, the greatest impact is to be had at the top of the scale. Note, however, that if the person asking is more senior, and he or she chooses to use the final example, this demonstrates that he or she is happy not exercising the power both parties know exists. This is, in itself, a form of confidence.

What is your language saying? By using your default language, you may be sending out subliminal messages. Monitor your language and that of your colleagues. How do you compare?

NEVER MAKE A DEFENCE OR AN APOLOGY UNTIL YOU ARE ACCUSED.

King Charles I

Self-deprecation vs Self-promotion

Women may be more prone to lack confidence and be unwilling to assert themselves, probably because of sexual stereotyping of roles during their childhood and education.

In general, women are socialised to downplay their certainties, whilst men are socialised to minimise their doubts.

Imagine, after giving a speech, a woman saying, 'I don't think my speech went very well'.
Depending on whom she spoke to, she might get two very different responses:
Female colleague: 'I thought that you were great'.
Male colleague: 'You could always get coaching'.

In this example, the woman is looking for affirmation whereas the man thinks that she is looking for advice.

Apologising

Women tend to apologise more than men and have a lower threshold regarding what warrants an apology. Perhaps what is significant is what women are apologising for. Most notable of these is a tendency to apologise for disagreeing.

You could either say, for example, 'I'm sorry, but I am going to have to disagree with you there'. Or you could say, 'I disagree'.

Since disagreement is arguably the only way to achieve a democratic culture, no one should apologise for it. You can find other ways, such as using framing language, to soften the impact of a disagreement and establish rapport.

INTONATION

- A rising intonation is suggestive of a question and potentially doubt.
- A flat intonation is suggestive of a statement.
- A lowering intonation suggests command.

Dealing with Aggression

Constructive disagreement is one of the foundations of a healthy and productive working environment. Conflict and aggression are the antithesis of it, however.

We all have to deal with conflict and we all have a particular way of dealing with it. It's helpful to understand how you, as well as other people, tend to respond to conflict.

Bear in mind that we all vary our approach depending on a number of factors: our mood, the contentiousness of the topic, whether we're dealing with colleagues or clients, our particular history with the person with whom we have the conflict.

'Conflict situations' are those in which the concerns of two people appear to be incompatible. In such situations, we can describe an individual's behaviour in two dimensions:

- Assertiveness, the extent to which the person attempts to satisfy his/her own concerns

- Cooperativeness, the extent to which the person attempts to satisfy the other person's concerns.

These two basic dimensions of behaviour define five different modes for responding to conflict situations:

1 COMPETING
In this style of conflict, neither side will back down. This approach is useful in court and in war. Some people describe it as a zero-sum game. It is assertive and uncooperative – an individual pursues his or her own concerns at the other person's expense.

2 ACCOMMODATING
This is the conflict style of the diplomat or facilitator. It is unassertive and cooperative – the complete opposite of competing. Typically it is observed when one side is prepared to give up completely on something small in order to negotiate a bigger deal later.

When accommodating, the individual neglects their own concerns to satisfy the concerns of the other person. There is an element of self-sacrifice in this mode. Accommodating might take the form of selfless generosity or charity, obeying another person's order when you would prefer not to, or yielding to another's point of view.

③ AVOIDING
This conflict style is unassertive and uncooperative. The person neither pursues his or her own concerns nor those of the other individual. They therefore do not actually deal with the conflict. Avoiding might take the form of diplomatically sidestepping an issue, postponing an issue until a better time, or simply withdrawing from a threatening situation.

④ COLLABORATING
This conflict style requires both sides to adopt it in order to be effective. This works well in an environment in which everyone can see the bigger picture. Collaborating can be described as both assertive and cooperative – the complete opposite of avoiding.

⑤ COMPROMISING
Compromising can be characterised as 'you give a bit, I give a bit – we both benefit'. The objective is to find some expedient, mutually acceptable solution that partially satisfies both parties. It falls between competing and accommodating.

Compromising gives up more than competing but less than accommodating. It addresses an issue more directly than avoiding does, but it does not explore it in as much depth as collaborating.

It is worth noting that all strategies are valid. We develop them as children and each of us is capable of using all five conflict-handling modes. None of us can be characterised as having a single style of dealing with conflict, but certain people use some modes better than others and, therefore, tend to rely on those modes more heavily than others – whether because of temperament or practice.

> NEVER RUIN AN APOLOGY WITH AN EXCUSE.
> BENJAMIN FRANKLIN

Perceptual positioning

Your conflict behaviour in the workplace is a result of both your personal predispositions and the requirements of the situation in which you find yourself. No one style will fit every circumstance – and smart people are flexible and can spot the right style for the right moment.

There are two sides to every argument, and sometimes even more than that. The idea of perceptual positioning is that in any argument you can take one of three positions: your view, the aggressor's view and a third (neutral) view.

The problem with responding to aggression by taking an entrenched position is that you may miss an opportunity to see your error, and you may not fully comprehend the nature of your aggressor's challenge and the possible legitimacy of the wider issues it evokes.

If you are flexible and try to understand other people's positions, you will be more empathetic, and you might even find constructive ways of changing your own opinion. Adopting the third, neutral, stance is an excellent tool for mediating disagreement and judging the situation objectively.

HONEST DISAGREEMENT IS OFTEN A GOOD SIGN OF PROGRESS.

Mahatma Gandhi

CHAPTER 20

Networking & Relationship Building

Many networking opportunities are not the obvious drinks parties. Conversations in the lift, while greeting clients or waiting for a meeting to start, are excellent opportunities for professional interactions.

Be aware that your day will be littered with opportunities to consolidate your own professional network. You may also find ways of enhancing your business's reputation and building important relationships.

Once you have established a friendly, personal relationship, you will be able to talk directly – this can be a good way of gaining intelligence about upcoming networking events, business initiatives and so on.

Brand Ambassador

Remember that, at any corporate event, you are acting as a brand ambassador, and you're therefore out to impress. Retain your professional gloss at all times. It goes without saying that you will never say anything negative about your company.

You're representing your company, so it is a good idea to have a short 'pitch' prepared: explain what your company does, what it aspires to do and what your role is within the company. Give information about new products, policies or initiatives.

You must also be adept at fielding prying or provocative remarks. Politely and confidently change the subject and move on. If caught unawares, it's best to feign ignorance rather than to give out misinformation. You may also be asked questions to which you do not know the answer. It is best to be honest and say politely, 'I'm not the best person to answer that'.

Remember to follow up contacts. If you meet someone who might make a good contact, exchange business cards or contact details, send an email within the next few days, saying how pleased you were to meet them.

IF YOU WANT TO GO FAST GO ALONE. IF YOU WANT TO GO FAR GO WITH OTHERS.

African Proverb

Networking Events

Building your network will facilitate professional interactions that may further your career and advance the fortunes of the company you work for. It can also be a way of introducing stimulating new ideas and innovative connections to your working life.

As a representative of your company you will be involved in supporting and reinforcing your networking. You will also come across many instances where it is useful for you to do your own networking.

For many people, entering a roomful of strangers and maximising the networking opportunities on offer can be a daunting prospect, but there are several strategies that will help.

1. **Wear the Tag**
   Nametags are very useful as they enable you to assess and identify strangers, and prioritise who you approach.

2. **Set Your Goals**
   Identify your networking goals – they could range from obtaining sales leads to making contacts, or just being a good brand ambassador – and adhere to them.

3. **Make your Approach**
   People will be grateful if you initiate contact and advance towards them with your hand outstretched. It's best to approach groups of three or more. Avoid interrupting two people who are deep in conversation, and be wary of people on their own as you might become trapped.

4. **Start a Conversation**
   Simple questions – 'Have you come far?', 'What company do you work for?', 'What did you think of the presentation?' – will get the ball rolling. Don't be afraid of small talk; if the conversation is flagging, fall back on safe topics such as weather, traffic or sporting events.

5. **Focus**
   Never be caught looking around the room for better prospects when you're mid-conversation. Even if you feel that the person you're talking to doesn't have much to offer, see the conversation out and make a polite exit: 'I suppose I/we ought to circulate now'. Don't be embarrassed – working the room is normal, and expected, behaviour at networking events.

MAKE IT COUNT

There will be many occasions when you are called upon to explain yourself, your role, your company or your executive. Anticipate the enquiry, prepare for all contingencies and really make that moment count.

1 Research
Whenever you're meeting a client – whether it's in a formal situation or a brief conversation as you wait for the lift – try to prepare beforehand. Establish their correct name, their role and position, and the nature of their business. Use this knowledge to address them appropriately.

2 Prepare a mission statement
What are the key messages that you want to get across about your company? You may find guidance in your company's brand guidelines, for example a series of key words that eloquently express your company's business philosophy. Familiarise yourself and be confident that you can get the right message across.

3 Keep it general
You've only got a few minutes to make an impact, so don't allow yourself to become sidetracked by specific questions or detailed discussions.

4 Pitch it for the occasion
If you're talking to a client at a corporate event and they're asking you questions about the company then it's fine to adhere to your mission statement. But if you're walking someone to a meeting room, the opportunity is limited. Try to get just one key point across.

5 Small talk
When encounters are very fleeting, you may find that reverting to friendly small talk is the best way to make an impact. You will be acting as a brand ambassador, and if you're friendly and courteous you will make a positive impact, which reflects on your company and your senior management.

6 Listen carefully
When you're meeting more than one client (for example, if you're sitting in a meeting room waiting for attendees to arrive), it can be very revealing to listen to their conversation. Even if they're not talking about business, you may be able to gather some important information about their relationships, their personalities, interests and pastimes.

7 Be observant
Observe carefully, whether you're in a formal meeting or an informal encounter. Look at body language, interaction with other people, and demeanour. All these observations may ultimately be useful.

8 Make a record
Every contact with a client or customer is significant, so always think about your CRM (customer relationship management) data. Ensure that any information you have gleaned is added to your database promptly.

What is a CRM Database?

This is a way of collecting and accessing information about customers or clients – it can span a range of business activities, from sales records, to enquiries and complaints.

Depending on the nature of your business, a typical CRM database will contain the following information:

- Personal details of the customer (email, phone number etc). Record recommended forms of address (Ms, Mrs etc), or any personal preferences.

- Source of leads (how did the customer get in touch with the company? (social media, email, website, personal referral etc).

- Interactions made with the customer (the last time they were in contact, when they last submitted feedback or a complaint, when they last requested information etc).

- Purchase history: detailed reports will be very revealing about customers' buying habits, and will help you to identify general trends.

- Other information: any data that will help you maintain a friendly relationship with the customer – number of children, holiday plans, favourite hobbies or pastimes.

My own business always bores me to death; I prefer other people's.

Oscar Wilde

CHAPTER 21

Business Entertaining & Travel

Offering hospitality to clients and customers is very much the same as hosting in private life. If you are the instigator, you must take your hosting duties seriously and use traditional courtesy and etiquette to charm your guests and put them at their ease.

Similarly, if you are invited for a business lunch, you must put every effort into being an appreciative guest, taking your lead from your host at all times.

It goes without saying that hosts and guests should put their mobile phones away, and keep them on silent throughout the meal. If there is an urgent reason for being alert to an incoming phone call, you must explain why to the table at large – in these circumstances the phone should still be kept out of view, preferably in a pocket.

For both parties, punctuality is key. Don't fall into the lazy habit of texting to say you've been held up. Your friends may well tolerate this behaviour, but it looks slapdash and disrespectful in a business context.

Always remain mindful of the difference between socialising and business entertaining. No matter how well you get on with your colleagues, clients or boss, working relationships are transactional, and your behaviour will be judged accordingly. Getting drunk, greedily consuming mountains of food, or outstaying your welcome are all social sins that may count against you in a business context.

Offering Hospitality

Business lunches are an intrinsic part of business culture, and are seen as an excellent way of wooing new clients or customers, or showing heartfelt gratitude for services rendered.

If you are organising the lunch, follow these simple recommendations:

- Choose a venue that you are familiar with, and book in advance. Do your best to secure a table that is not near the cloakrooms, and avoid tables that face a mirror. If you have an odd number of guests try to secure a round table, so that nobody has to sit next to an empty chair.

- When you are organising the seating, put the most honoured, important or distinguished guest to the right of the host; the second-highest ranking guest should be to the left of the host, and so on (alternating right and left). Unlike with social occasions, there is no imperative to alternate genders; status is much more important in a business context.

- Arrive early. If it is possible to wait in a lobby or reception area for your guests, then do so. If you are ushered to your table, take your seat, and rise to your feet when each guest arrives, remaining standing until they are seated. The normal business greeting is to shake hands.

- When it comes to ordering drink, indicate that your guest/s can have whatever they like, saying something like 'Would you like a drink? Wine? Mineral water? Or something stronger?'.

> ONCE A MONTH, GO TO LUNCH WITH SOMEONE WHO KNOWS MORE ABOUT YOUR BUSINESS THAN YOU DO.
> H JACKSON BROWN JR

- If your guests decline an alcoholic drink, it's acceptable for you to order, say, a glass of wine, but leave it at that.

- When it comes to ordering food, you can either gently guide your guests through the menu, making recommendations, and indicating whether you will be ordering a starter and so on, or you can give them free rein; if they are left to their own devices, you will have to mirror the number of courses they order to make them feel comfortable.

- If the party is going to drink wine, then it is your job to order for the table. Note what your guests have ordered and in most circumstances you will find it expedient to order both red and white wine. It is perfectly acceptable to opt for the house wine; if you wish to make more of a lavish gesture and are unsure about what to order, call over the sommelier (or your waiter) and ask for advice, preferably encouraging him/her to point out recommendations on the wine list, so you can see the prices.

- Observe your guests' drinks and if it looks like glasses are empty, summon a waiter to replenish their glasses, or ask if they'd like another drink. You must be attentive to your guests' needs at all times.

- Save any business talk for later in proceedings. The first part of the meal should be about general chat, pleasantries, and getting to know your guests. It is only after this procedure that you can get down to business.

- When the bill arrives, deal with it smoothly and discreetly – a quick glimpse at the total and a swiftly brandished credit card is ideal. It might be wise to enquire about service charges when booking, or before your guests arrive, so your guests don't have to witness awkward 'does this include a tip?' exchanges.

- Signal the end of the meal by placing your napkin on the table and rising from your chair.

Receiving Business Hospitality

As a guest, you need to be alert to your host's behaviour and read any signals carefully. If you are offered a drink before the meal and you're not sure what the protocol is, you can always say something like 'I'll start with a mineral water'. If it turns out to be a bibulous lunch, you can always drink wine later.

It is quite likely that the host will give you some guidance as to choosing from the menu; if you're really stuck you can always say something like 'It all looks so delicious, I don't know what to choose. What are you having?/What do you recommend?'

Don't over-order – doggedly working your way through three hefty courses is not a good look. You don't want your business associates to think you're greedy. If the lunch is to comprise several courses, make sure that you order, for example, a light starter.

Beware challenging and messy foods. Being highly attuned to the subtleties of a business relationship while desperately trying to demolish a grouse or extract the flesh from a lobster is a multi-tasking nightmare.

You may be called upon to talk or answer questions when you're dining in a business context. Never do so with your mouth full. If you have just taken a mouthful when you're asked a question, smile and flap your hand at your mouth, or hold up a finger to indicate you'll be just a moment, before swallowing.

Remember your ps and qs. It is obvious that you must be extremely polite to your host, but also saying please and thank you to waiters and waitresses, besides being common courtesy, makes you look attentive and gracious.

When you get back to the office, drop your host a quick email thanking them for the meal and his/her hospitality. Do this promptly (preferably the same day).

THERE'S NO SUCH THING AS A FREE LUNCH.

Milton Friedman

Business Travel

If you're going on a business trip with colleagues, you may feel that the lines of traditional office etiquette are being redrawn: you may suddenly find yourself snoozing next to a colleague on a plane, eating breakfast with them, or even sunbathing together by the hotel pool. But don't be fooled by the enforced intimacy of the trip; work hierarchies still exist.

It will be much more relaxing if you can travel to and from your destination separately from your colleagues. Other people may want to do things separately from you – for example arriving at the airport hours before departure or sleeping through the entire flight – and separate travel arrangements will avoid any embarrassment.

Once you're at the hotel, you may need to find excuses to avoid unremitting proximity to your colleagues. You can always plead that you need time to make phone calls or do some work in your room. Alternatively, you can play the exercise card – if the hotel has a swimming pool or gym you may be able to get away from your colleagues for a couple of precious hours.

If you're on a solo trip, don't be afraid to dine alone in a hotel restaurant, but try not to feel self-conscious about your solitude. A book, newspaper or phone can provide distraction, or you can simply sit back and indulge in some discreet people-watching.

> A MAN OF ORDINARY TALENT WILL ALWAYS BE ORDINARY, WHETHER HE TRAVELS OR NOT; BUT A MAN OF SUPERIOR TALENT WILL GO TO PIECES IF HE REMAINS FOREVER IN THE SAME PLACE...
> WOLFGANG AMADEUS MOZART

How to Handle Business Travel

- Arrive at every meeting, venue etc on time.
  It will show that you are respectful of your host's time, and will be appreciated (if not always practised) in every culture.

- Adapt to local customs.
  This means researching beforehand and being observant on your arrival. Follow your hosts' leads at all times to avoid embarrassing *faux-pas*, especially around touching, greeting and body language.

- Dress appropriately.
  You will need to look respectable at all times, and that involves doing some research beforehand and understanding local customs. Play safe by choosing clothes that cover your knees and shoulders.

- Don't criticise.
  No matter what the provocation, it is rude to comment negatively on your host country's infrastructure or bureaucracy. Your hosts may well find their own country's institutions infuriating, but criticising them is solely their prerogative.

- Be discreet.
  Keep business conversations private and don't gossip about the reasons for your trip to casual acquaintances – be aware that they may not have your best interests at heart.

- Negotiate intelligently.
  You will need to research the business etiquette of the country you are visiting beforehand, so that you can effectively gauge the atmosphere in the meeting, and adjust your behaviour. Always aim for assertiveness without aggression.

- Watch your table manners.
  Again, research into each country's customs and traditions is essential. Even if your hosts' table manners leave something to be desired – for example chatting on their mobiles during the meal – don't let your own standards slip and remember you are acting as an ambassador for your company.

Afterword

Business etiquette covers most of the everyday practicalities of office life. It's simply a code of manners that helps to regulate how people behave in an office setting. It's not just about standing up when certain people enter the room, or who should sit first when a group goes into a meeting. It's about how to behave towards clients on the phone – including rude ones – how to communicate and what to communicate, how to make an excuse for lateness and how to deal with that excuse, how to introduce clients to colleagues, how to give and take criticism, when and how to organise a business lunch, how to treat colleagues, and what to wear.

It's about making sure that, whatever the occasion, we perform in a way that reflects positively on ourselves and our place of work. And we are most likely to perform to the best of our ability if we have some good idea of what is expected of us, and by whom and why.

The world of work is dynamic and evolving. Vestiges of old structures and hierarchies linger on in the most traditional institutions, but for the most part the onset of the digital age has brought rapid transformations. We have addressed new innovations, such as video conferencing, home working and instant messaging, in *Debrett's Guide To Business Etiquette*.

Working environments continue to adapt to changing social attitudes and to the challenges we face in today's world. The Covid pandemic that swept across the globe in 2020 radically disrupted old working patterns. It remains to be seen whether some of the more progressive adaptations – for example the rise of 'digital nomads', who can work on a laptop from anywhere in the world with reliable WiFi – will remain, or whether there will be a slow reversion to the old norms.

At Debrett's we continue to monitor the changing world of work, and the Business Etiquette section of our website (www.debretts.com) will be continually updated. We rely on our readers, who are experiencing the world of work in all its many facets, to keep us informed about new trends, practices and etiquette challenges. So if you would like to join the conversation, please contact us at editors@debretts.co.uk.

DON'T JUDGE EACH DAY BY THE HARVEST YOU REAP BUT BY THE SEEDS THAT YOU PLANT.

Robert Louis Stevenson

INDEX

Agendas, meeting 156–157
Aggression, dealing with 202–203
Apologising 201
Applications, for jobs 19, 22
Appointments, being in time 57
Body language 31, 192–194
Brand ambassador 207
Bullying 76–77
Business cards 39, 129
Business entertaining 213–217
Business hospitality, receiving 216
Business letters 123–125
Business lunch 213–214
    ordering food 215
    ordering wine 215
    paying the bill 215
    seating plan 214
Business Travel 218–219
    dress 219
    etiquette 219
    greetings 219
    punctuality 219
    table manners 219
Chairperson, duties 157
Communication, general 99–105
    email 115–119
    language 101
    letters 123–125
    purpose 99, 104
    written or spoken 103
Communication, gender differences 199
Complaints 137–143
    dealing with 141
    formal 143
    from third parties 137
    from within the office 140
    incoming 138
    informal 142
    outgoing 138–139
Compliments slips 128
Correspondence, business 121–129
    business letters, layout 124–125
    envelopes 126
    headed notepaper 126
    letter-writing 121
    replying to letters 124

    salutations 123
    sign offs 123
Covering letter (with CV) 19, 21, 22
Criticism 144–145
    giving 133, 144
    taking 145
CRM database 211
Curriculum Vitae (CV) 19, 20–21
Cyberbullying 76
Digital nomads 220
Dismissal 135, 145–50
Dress codes, office 63–66
Emails 115–119
    cc and bcc 116
    punctuation and language 116
    reply vs reply all 118
    responding to emails 121
    salutations and sign offs 118
    subject line/importance label 115
    threads and attachments 119
Envelopes 126
Excuses, for being late 58, 60–61
Eye contact 170, 190–191
Favours, asking 105
Faxes 128
First impressions 186–187
Forgetting names 39
Formal complaints 143
Formality 49
Friendships, work 69–70
Gossip 78–81
Grooming 66
Handshakes 35
Harassment 77
Headed notepaper 126
Home office 17
Home working 13, 14–15
Hot desk syndrome 13
Hot desking 11, 12–13
Ideas, presenting 48, 56
Informal complaints 142
Interviews 19, 24–33,
    acceptable topics 26
    afterwards 29
    asking questions 26
    body language 31
    concluding 27
    conducting 24

dress 65
location 25
offering refreshments 27
video 32–33
Interviewee behaviour 28
Introducing people 37–39
Introductions, formal 38
Introductions, VIPs 40
Jargon 101
Kissing, social 37
Latecomers, how to deal with them 60
Leaving parties 90
Leaving presents 91
Meetings 153–165
    agendas 156–157
    attending 160
    formal 159–160
    ninutes 162–163
    preparation 153
    venue 155
Memos 102
Minutes, meeting 162–163
Mobile phones, in business 95, 113
Networking 207–211
Networking events 209
New staff 52–56
    how to behave 55–56
    monitoring 52
    offering help 52
    welcoming 51–52
Office romance 72–75
Office, 8–17, 42–55, 62–91
    bullying 76–77
    culture 9, 45, 52
    dress 63–66
    friendships 69–70
    hierarchies 49
    manners 43
    parties 84–86
    privacy 11
    romance 72–75
    socialising 83–91
    space 11,
On-screen etiquette 33
Perceptual positioning 204
Phones 106–113
    answering 107
    difficult calls 112

making calls 109
mobiles 113
privacy 93
terminating calls 112
unwanted calls 111
voicemail, messages 111
Praise, giving 104
Privacy 93, 97
Public speaking 167–183
    fear of 169
Punctuality 57–61
    dealing with latecomers 60
    letting people know 58
Redundancy 145–150
Reports, written 134
Review Board 133
Reviews, annual 131–135
Rumours 81
Self-deprecation 201
Self-promotion 201
Senior staff, gaining access to 50
Shyness, overcoming 190
Smiling 170, 187–188
Social media 96
Socialising, work 83–91
Soft skills 185–197
Speeches and presentations 167–183
    delivering a presentation 176
    duration 175
    language 178
    notes 172
    pausing and silence 171
    persuasion 179
    preparation 172–173
    questions & answers 182–183
    structure 174
    visuals, use of 180
Team building 46
Team spirit, socialising 83
Teamwork 45
Thank you, saying 47
Video calls 17, 164
Video interviews 32–33
Video meetings 164–165
Video mistakes 165
Voicemail 111
Working lunch 88–89